Perception isn't only about the perceiver.

This book shows what it passes through.

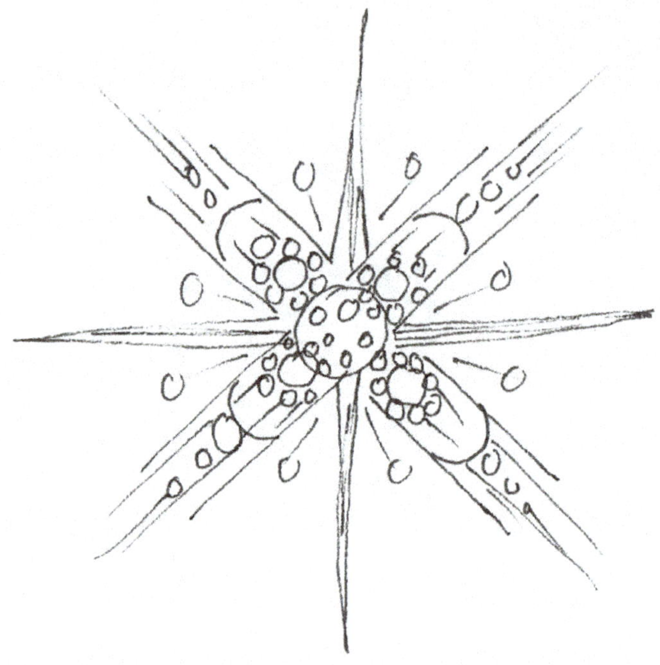

First Edition, 2026.
BioMind Superpowers Books.
ISBN-13: 978-1-949214-93-2

You Know More Than You Think
A Five-Book Series

Book Five
The Gravity of Reality
Explorations in the Weight of Thought

Elly Flippen

A BIOMIND SUPERPOWERS BOOK
PUBLISHED BY

Swann-Ryder Productions, LLC

DISCLAIMER

This book is provided for informational, educational, and experiential purposes only. It is not intended as medical, psychological, psychiatric, therapeutic, legal, or scientific advice, nor should it be used as a substitute for professional diagnosis, treatment, or consultation.

The author is affiliated with Swann-Ryder Productions, LLC, which holds certain copyrights and related intellectual property rights to the published and unpublished writings and artwork of Ingo Swann. This book may reference, quote, or discuss his published material for educational and contextual purposes. All interpretations, analyses, applications, and contemporary extensions presented herein are solely those of the author.

Nothing in this book should be interpreted as representing official positions of any scientific, governmental, institutional, or research organization. References to perception research, anomalous experience, or non-ordinary awareness are included for historical, educational, and phenomenological exploration.

This work does not claim to prove, validate, or guarantee the existence of paranormal, psychic, extrasensory, or supernatural abilities, nor does it present such phenomena as scientifically established fact.

Individual experiences will vary. No guarantees are made regarding outcomes, results, insights, or personal transformation.

Readers are responsible for their own engagement with the material and for their physical, emotional, and psychological well-being. Individuals with a history of trauma, dissociation, significant mental health conditions, neurological or cardiovascular concerns, or other medical conditions should consult a qualified healthcare professional before engaging in any practices described.

The practices described in this book are voluntary exercises intended for personal exploration and should be approached with discretion and self-awareness.

While reasonable efforts have been made to ensure the accuracy of the information presented, the author and Swann-Ryder Productions, LLC assume no responsibility for errors or omissions and make no warranties regarding the completeness, reliability, or applicability of the material.

By choosing to engage with this book, the reader accepts responsibility for its use and for any decisions or actions arising from the material presented.

READER GUIDANCE

The following guidance is offered to support safe, grounded, and thoughtful engagement with the practices and explorations presented in this book.

Readers are encouraged to:

> Move at a pace that feels appropriate and sustainable.
> Modify, pause, or discontinue any practice that creates discomfort, distress, or instability.
> Seek qualified professional support when encountering intense emotional, psychological, or perceptual experiences.

The material in this book is not intended to replace sound judgment, professional care, or responsible engagement with daily life, relationships, and decision-making.

These practices are offered as invitations to explore awareness and perceptual literacy, not as doctrines of belief, systems of authority, or substitutes for medical, psychological, or therapeutic care.

Your consent, grounding, safety, and discernment are foundational to your engagement with the material presented here.

TABLE OF CONTENTS

HOW TO APPROACH THIS BOOK

This volume is not a sequence of techniques to master.

It is meant to be entered, tested in life, and returned to as your perception integrates into movement, decision, and relationship.

In earlier books, information was something to notice, stabilize, and integrate.

Here, information encounters limits that do not resolve through skill or insight alone.

The discovery is no longer how to access your awareness.

It is how to remain oriented when your awareness cannot move freely.

Some sections may feel immediately applicable. Others may feel indirect or unresolved.

That is expected.

In this phase, understanding often appears after contact, not before it.

What matters is not forcing clarity but noticing how your awareness organizes when it meets real situations without being driven toward conclusion.

PERMEABILITY AS A
CONDITION OF AWARENESS

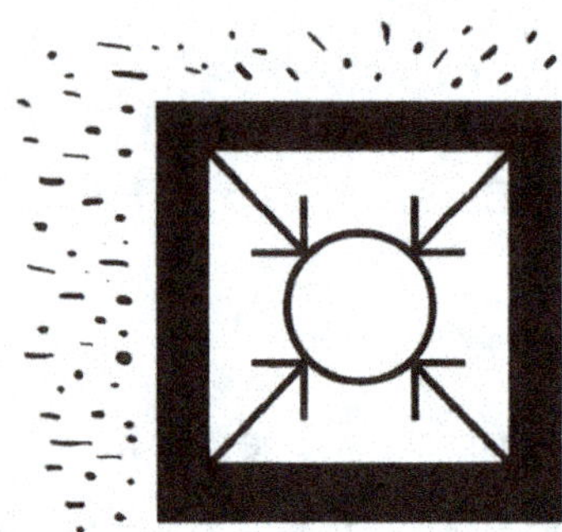

NON-PERMEABLE

- Reduced thresholds of awareness
- Limited capacity to hold unresolved information

PERMEABLE

- Expanded thresholds of awareness
- Greater capacity to hold unresolved information

When thresholds are **rigid**, awareness narrows.
When thresholds are **flexible**, awareness
can tolerate ambiguity.

On Permeability & Awareness

The diagram on the previous page is adapted from an early model presented by Ingo.

It is not offered as a theory to adopt or a distinction to enforce.

It points to a simple dynamic:

> Awareness does not register everything equally.
> It is shaped by thresholds.

When thresholds are rigid, your awareness narrows.

When thresholds are flexible, your awareness can tolerate ambiguity, novelty, and unresolved information.

This does not make one orientation superior to another. It makes them different in what they can hold.

Earlier in this series, attention was described as the force that energizes what it treats as significant and de-energizes what it treats as insignificant.

Here, that same mechanism appears one step earlier.

What becomes significant is not determined only by personal attention.

It is shaped by what information is permitted to register in the first place.

Social norms, identity structures, plausibility limits, and cultural consensus do not usually block signals outright.

They adjust the permeability of what one can be aware of.

Nothing dramatic occurs. Information simply fails to organize.

This is not ignorance. It is not deception. It is a condition of orientation.

The material herein explores what happens when these thresholds are shaped collectively, and how your awareness can remain coherent even when it cannot advance freely.

The diagram is not meant to be analyzed.

Its relevance often becomes clear later, when something in your experience gains or loses weight, urgency, or legitimacy without an obvious internal cause.

When that happens, return here.

GETTING READY

Before engaging the explorations, it helps to understand how this material is meant to be used.

This section is not a set of cautions or instructions. It is an orientation.

The chapters that follow examine how your awareness is shaped, limited, or redirected by social, cultural, and structural forces. These influences often operate before conscious choice.

Nothing here requires effort, special states, or pushing you beyond what feels natural.

What you perceive remains most reliable when it is allowed to register without demand for conclusion.

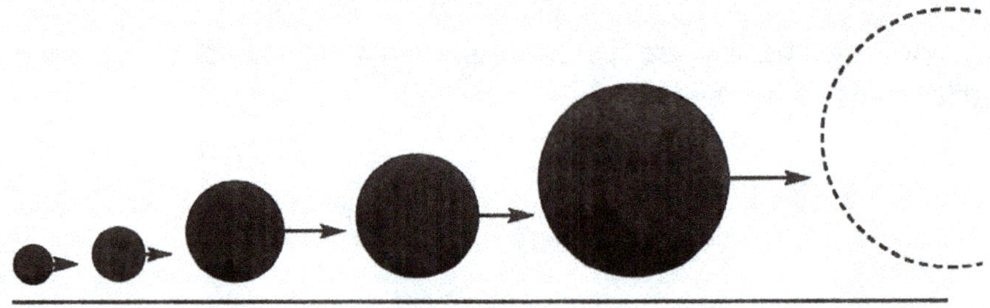

DEVELOPMENT

The Role of Diagrams, Explorations, & Pauses

The diagrams in this book are not models to adopt or systems to believe. They are reference points for dynamics you may already recognize.

The explorations are not techniques to perform correctly. They also includes *What to Watch For* and reflection questions.

> *What to Watch For* points are not predictions or guarantees. They are orientation cues, examples of how shifts may appear, so they are less likely to be overlooked.
> *Reflection* questions are not meant to be answered correctly. They are invitations to remain with your experience long enough for it to clarify. If other questions arise, you are encouraged to follow them as well.

Each exploration is a temporary orientation, not a state to remain in. Enter deliberately. Observe what becomes noticeable. Then exit.

When an exploration concludes, return to baseline: your body, your surroundings, and the ordinary rhythms of daily life.

Integration does not come from sustaining an altered orientation. It comes from noticing how your system interacts in lived situations.

If something feels effortful, destabilizing, or mentally gripping, pause. Ground. Let your system relax.

In this territory, restraint restores clarity faster than persistence.

Throughout the book you will encounter brief pauses labeled:

> Pause. Check resonance.
> What you're noticing.

These are not prompts to analyze or interpret.

The question is not: *What does this mean?*

And not even: *What am I perceiving?*

It is simply:

Am I still oriented?

> Silence is a valid response.
> Neutrality is information.
> Lack of signal is also a signal.

Staying Grounded While Living from Perception

Grounding remains essential, not as precaution, but as a condition for usable awareness. As signal encounters compression, authority, or collective certainty, clarity depends on remaining embodied and internally oriented. If your awareness begins to feel inflated, pressured, emotionally compelled, identity-forming, or subtly unsafe, return to what is most basic:

> breath
> posture
> physical sensation
> connection with the room

These simple anchors help restore orientation before interpretation takes hold.

Additional reset practices are available in the Appendix and can be used whenever grounding needs to be reestablished.

Clarity begins in the body. Organismic intelligence depends on grounding. It does not override it. If you experience persistent anxiety, disorientation, or difficulty remaining present in ordinary life, pause your engagement and return to familiar routines.

Pausing is not failure; it is perceptual maturity.

Final Orientation Before Beginning

This book is not about becoming oppositional, enlightened, or correct.

Earlier in this series, you were introduced to the ideas of mind-maps and reality boxes: the internal and cultural structures that silently shape what is noticed, what is dismissed, and what appears meaningful.

In this volume, those ideas expand. The focus shifts from how perception organizes within you to how attention, authority, and collective structures shape what becomes visible at all. As perceptual maturity deepens, it tends to:

> reduce certainty rather than inflate it
> soften urgency
> quiet dramatic interpretation
> increase discernment without withdrawal

You are not registering perception in order to become something new.

You are discovering how to remain yourself while your attention, significance, and power interact.

THE WEIGHT OF THOUGHT

PERCEPTION AT THE LIMITS

A Necessary Pause Before Awareness Meets Force

Across this series, the process has progressed in stages: first noticing what is already present, then stabilizing within movement, then recognizing the landscapes through which meaning takes form, and then embodying what becomes clear.

Book Five turns toward reckoning, not as punishment, but as gravity.

> What we notice shapes what we stabilize.
> What we stabilize shapes how meaning structures itself.
> What structures itself becomes lived.
> And what is lived carries consequence.

Reckoning is the moment information meets the weight of its own architecture, where belief, attention, and interpretation are no longer abstract, but forces that organize reality itself.

By the time you arrive here, your organismic intelligence is no longer theoretical. It has been practiced and refined.

The architecture you now examine is one you have already been inhabiting.

> You investigated how what you perceive registers in the body.
> You navigated through how emotional tone shapes meaning.
> You discovered how symbols arise, and how distortion enters when they are taken literally.
> You dove into how to hold your vantage point, so your awareness does not collapse into experience.

In Book Three, you explored how perception is organized within internal frames of reference that determine how your experience is interpreted and stabilized.

You mapped out how those frames can clarify, distort, or constrain what registers.

What remains now is not internal clarity. It is context: the structures through which clarity must pass.

Up to this point, the explorations have focused inwardly: how perception forms, stabilizes, differentiates, and integrates within a single system.

This book steps back to see the bigger picture. Not outward into abstraction, but outward into the conditions that shape what your awareness is allowed to notice, hold, and integrate in real life.

If Book Three examined these structures within the individual, Book Five examines their collective counterparts, and the broader environments within which perception unfolds.

Because your awareness does not operate in a vacuum.

It moves within:

> social agreements
> cultural norms
> identity structures
> power dynamics
> collective narratives
> unspoken rules about what is reasonable, credible, or safe to perceive
> explanatory frameworks that define what counts as real
> informational environments that guide what receives attention
> planetary conditions that form the physical context in which perception occurs

These influences rarely appear as force or coercion. They appear as normality, as what feels reasonable, realistic, or obvious, as what is sensible.

Normality is the most effective filter... because it does not feel like one.

What This Book Is

In Book Four, the central question was:

How do I live from what I am aware of without losing coherence?

Here, the question shifts:

What happens to information about what's already there when it encounters structures that limit perception itself?

These limits are not always personal. They are often shared. They do not announce themselves as suppression. They operate silently, upstream of thought, shaping what records, what fades, and what never fully appears, and how experience is translated so it can remain acceptable.

This is why people can be intelligent, sincere, and well-intentioned, and still fail to perceive what is directly in front of them.

This occurs not because information is missing, but because they are aware of itself is molded.

Book Five is about navigation under constraint. You will explore:

> how social permission shapes what awareness allows
> how plausibility filters compress perception
> how identity acts as a boundary on noticing
> how collective tone replaces internal orientation
> how taboo operates as inattention rather than fear
> how perceptual "black holes" form at scale
> how informational environments guide attention before interpretation begins
> how planetary and environmental conditions form part of the broader context of awareness
> how to remain oriented when your awareness is constrained
> how explanation reshapes your experience before it is evaluated

The emphasis is not on changing what you "see."

It is on holding orientation when "seeing" becomes difficult, constrained, translated, or impossible.

Why Power Appears Here

Where your awareness cannot move freely, your organismic intelligence cannot self-correct.

Where your organismic intelligence cannot self-correct, certainty, authority, and control tend to fill the gap.

This happens because power compensates for lost coherence, not because power is malicious.

The material herein explores this dynamic without blame:

> how perceptual limits scale from individuals to groups
> how "order" is preserved through narrowed awareness
> how rigidity forms without anyone intending harm
> how awareness can recognize collapse without being absorbed by it

This is not about overthrowing structure.

It is about noticing where structural forces replaces perception.

This Is Not a Critique of Society

This book is not an argument against culture, institutions, or power. It is not a call to rebellion, belief change, or withdrawal. It is a perceptual inquiry.

You will not be asked:

> to oppose systems
> to adopt new ideologies
> to replace one worldview with another

Instead, you will be invited to notice:

> when your awareness narrows before evaluation
> when your perception is filtered before it can be examined
> when your identity, plausibility, or social permission intervene
> when a collective tone replaces your internal reference
> when entire regions of experience disappear without resistance

These are not failures. They are adaptive mechanisms that once preserved coherence, and now inconspicuously limit it.

How to Approach What Follows

Move slowly.

> Do not rush toward conclusions.
> Do not look for villains.
> Do not turn perception into ideology.

Let the material function the way your perceptual awareness system itself does: cumulatively, and without demand.

You are not here to fix the world. You are here to remain coherent within it.

And that (when awareness meets force) is already enough.

What limits awareness is not lack of information, but the structure through which information must pass.

— Adapted from the perceptual models of Ingo Swann

---

22 | Cultural & Social Interference
When Shared Assumptions Shape What Awareness Allows

Opening Invitation

By this stage, perceptual coherence is no longer the primary challenge.

You have experienced how your awareness registers data, how meaning forms, and how distortion enters.

What becomes visible now is something fainter.

Not all limits on what registers arise from physiology, emotional charge, or cognitive noise.

Many arise from shared social conditioning.

These influences rarely feel imposed.

They feel like *common sense*.

The phrase *common sense* originally referred to a shared faculty, from the Latin *sensus communis*, meaning the "common sensing" that allows a community to perceive and judge reality together.

In early philosophical usage, it described the integrative capacity that coordinates the senses into a comprehensible picture of the world.

Over time, the term shifted. It came to mean what is widely agreed upon: what "everyone knows" without needing explanation.

In modern usage, common sense no longer describes a perceptual faculty. It describes consensus.

And consensus silently shapes what can be perceived.

Common sense defines:

> what you trust
> what you dismiss
> what you keep private
> what you never fully allow yourself to register

It does not typically forbid awareness outright.

It narrows what feels permissible.

This chapter explores how cultural, social, and identity-based assumptions function as perceptual governors, not blocking what you can be aware of entirely, but narrowing its usable range.

The aim here is not to oppose culture or dismantle belief.

It is to recognize when information is being filtered before you have had the opportunity to examine it directly.

Awareness of something makes its perception possible.

Without awareness of it, perception is not possible.

Consider this before beginning the material that follows.

Pause. Check resonance.

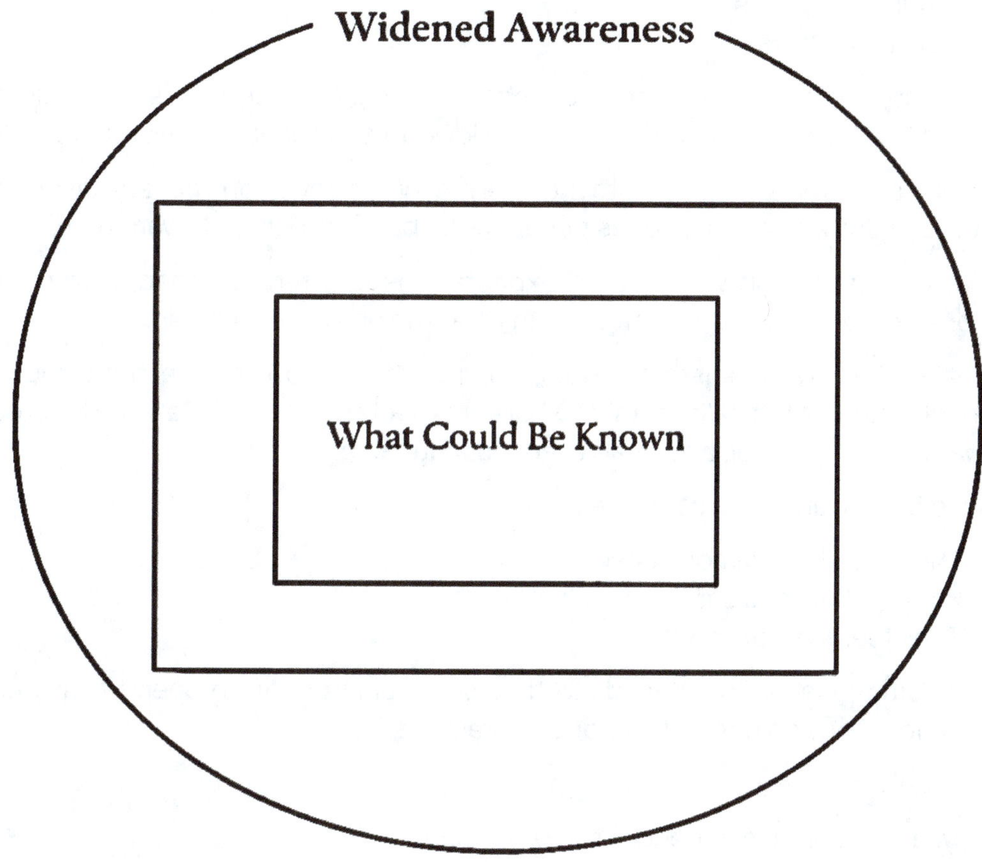

Widened Awareness
What Could Be Known

 ## The Nature of Societal Filters

Societal filters are not internal flaws or psychological defenses.

They are adaptive structures.

They develop because humans are social organisms and:

> belonging matters
> credibility matters
> stability matters

Over time, these priorities become embedded as pre-perceptual sieves: silent checks that occur before information is allowed into your active awareness.

Social systems naturally regulate themselves. When deviation appears, discreet equalizing forces emerge, not as punishment, but as pressure toward unity.

What does not align with shared expectations is often softened, reframed, ignored, or redirected until it fits within what the group can sustain.

Social systems resist sustained deviation: not through overt force, but through normalization. What falls outside shared expectation is gradually redirected toward what is familiar, acceptable, and manageable.

These forces rarely feel coercive.

> They feel like common sense.
> They feel like realism.
> They feel like maturity.

Unlike emotional or cognitive distortion, societal filters often operate without sensation. They do not feel charged or dramatic.

They feel normal.

Below are the primary categories you will map.

They are not as problems to fix, but instead are as patterns to recognize:

1. The Social Permission Filter
2. The Plausibility Filer
3. Identify Containment
4. The Cultural Echo
5. The Taboo Constraint

1. The Social Permission Filter

"Is it acceptable to notice this?"

This filter regulates what is perceivable through anticipated social response. Information is sorted not by accuracy, but by whether it feels safe to acknowledge. When this filter is active, information often registers cleanly, then disappears.

Common internal responses include:

> "That's probably nothing."
> "I shouldn't take that seriously."
> "There's no way to explain that."
> "Other people wouldn't see it this way."

The signal is not rejected because it is vague or weak. It is rejected because it feels socially inconvenient.

This filter is strongest in environments where:

> credibility is closely monitored
> rationality is equated with worth
> deviation risks exclusion
> ambiguity is discouraged
> social belonging depends on agreement

The intellect performs a rapid calculation: *If I notice this, who do I become in the eyes of others?*

What is perceived is then quietly edited to preserve:

> social standing
> professional identity
> group coherence
> internal alignment with "acceptable" ways of knowing

This process is usually unconscious. No explicit rule is broken. Nothing feels suppressed. Your attention simply turns away. The social permission filter does not distort perception. It prevents acknowledgment.

Clarity returns when a signal is allowed to transmit privately, without requiring immediate explanation, validation, or disclosure.

Organismic perception does not need permission to be accurate. It only needs space to exist before it is judged.

21

2. The Plausibility Filter
"Does this fit what I believe is possible?"

The plausibility filter equates truth with familiarity. Information is assessed not by its internal consistency or pattern, but by whether it conforms to established assumptions about how reality works.

When this filter is active, information is not rejected outright. It is reduced before it can take form.

Signals that fall outside established frameworks are:

> downgraded
> dismissed
> treated as coincidence
> deferred indefinitely
> never fully recorded

This process happens automatically and often feels reasonable. The intellect does not say, "This is impossible." It says nothing at all.

This is not skepticism. Skepticism examines information. The plausibility filter prevents information from organizing in the first place. Its function is adaptive.

It keeps what is perceived aligned with:

> cultural consensus
> shared explanatory models
> social credibility
> internal coherence

But the cost of this alignment is resolution.

When plausibility dominates:

> signals fade quickly
> anticipatory impressions fail to consolidate
> early pattern recognition dissolves before clarity forms
> data waits for confirmation that can only arrive later

The information was not wrong. It simply could not survive the filter.

Clarity returns when plausibility is treated as a secondary check rather than a gatekeeper. When information is allowed to organize first (and plausibility assessed later) your awareness expands without abandoning discernment.

What changes is not belief. It is sequence.

3. Identity Containment
"Is this consistent with who I am?"

Identity functions as a perceptual boundary. Roles, self-concepts, values, professional identities, and shared belief affiliations shape the range of what can enter your awareness.

Identity rarely forms in isolation. It often includes implicit statements such as:

> "I am a rational person."
> "I am a scientist."
> "I am spiritual."
> "I am part of this community."
> "People like us do not believe that.

When information appears that threatens identity coherence, it is rarely confronted directly.

More often, it is softened, reframed, rationalized, deferred, or ignored. This process is usually unconscious.

Its function is not deception, but stability.

Identity containment is especially strong in individuals and cultures that prioritize competence, rationality, authority, expertise, emotional control, social credibility, and/or belonging within a shared worldview.

When this filter is active:

> signal narrows to what fits the established self-image
> curiosity gives way to justification
> contradictory signals feel irrelevant rather than troubling
> coherence is preserved at the expense of accuracy

This filter does not create false perception. It limits its range.

Information that cannot be integrated into your identity does not disappear; it simply fails to organize into your awareness.

Clarity increases when your identity is held as context rather than constraint.

When the question shifts from "What does this say about me?" to "What is actually registering?", your organismic perception regains flexibility without threatening coherence.

Your identity remains intact while what you become aware of enlarges.

4. The Cultural Echo

"Everyone feels this... so it must be mine."

Groups generate shared emotional, attentional, and interpretive tone, a phenomenon explored earlier in this series through crowd dynamics, boundary load, and shared reality frames.

This tone is not imposed; it emerges naturally through proximity, shared focus, repetition, and reinforcement.

Without differentiation, shared atmosphere can be internalized as personal orientation. Mood, urgency, conviction, or concern can spread rapidly in:

> crowds
> workplaces
> families and social groups
> media environments
> periods of collective stress or uncertainty

This filter does not block information. It replaces internal reference points.

When the cultural echo is active:

> emotional tone feels compelling but not grounded
> certainty increases without corresponding clarity
> dissent or nuance feels uncomfortable or unnecessary
> perception aligns reflexively with the dominant signal

Because the experience feels shared, it often goes unquestioned.

The issue is not influence itself, but loss of differentiation.

Clarity returns when context is recognized as context, and what is collective can be perceived without being absorbed.

Your awareness regains its footing when the question shifts from "What is happening?" to "Where is this coming from?"

Cultural echoes weaken when your attention reorients to your body, baseline emotional tone, and present-moment grounding, allowing shared atmosphere to be registered without becoming your identity.

Pause. Check resonance.

5. The Taboo Constraint
"This is not something one notices."

Some forms of awareness are culturally discouraged without being explicitly forbidden.

They are not labeled as wrong.

Instead, they are framed as irrelevant, unserious, or inappropriate to acknowledge.

In everyday life, taboos often refer to subjects that are uncomfortable to discuss, such as money, politics, religion, sex, death, mental health, or bodily processes.

But the constraint often begins earlier than speech.

It shapes what people allow themselves to notice in the first place, including perceptions related to those very topics.

For example, noticing:

⟩   forms of knowing that precede explanation
⟩   relational or emotional dynamics
⟩   power and structural influence
⟩   socially sensitive domains

In many environments these perceptions are quietly dismissed.

This filter rarely appears as fear or resistance; more often it appears as inattention.

Your system simply learns that noticing certain things carries no social legitimacy.

As a result:

⟩   your attention disengages,
⟩   your awareness does not stabilize, and
⟩   a perception never fully forms.

Because nothing dramatic happens, this constraint is easy to miss.

Your organismic intelligence is not challenged.

It is quietly bypassed.

Pause. Check resonance.

EXPLORATION 22.1: The Social Permission Check
The Pull Toward Acceptability

Objective

To observe when your attention narrows in response to anticipated social judgment.

Setup

Recall a recent moment when you noticed something others apparently did not, but chose not to speak or act on it.

Steps

1. Bring the moment to mind lightly.
2. Ask: *What did I initially notice?*
3. Then ask: *When did my attention turn away from it?*
4. Notice what seemed to trigger the shift. For example:
    → fear of appearing foolish
    → concern about credibility
    → desire to appear rational or composed
    → uncertainty about social permission to acknowledge it
5. Do not correct anything. Simply notice how your attention reorganized.

What to Watch For

⟩ a moment of contraction when imagining others' opinions
⟩ relief when the social pressure is recognized
⟩ steadiness returning when the perception is allowed to exist privately

Reflection

↺ What shifted first: the perception itself, or concern about how it would be received?
↺ What identity or role felt at risk in that moment (competent, rational, agreeable)?
↺ If no one else were involved, would the perception have required action, or simply acknowledgment?
↺ What happened when you allowed the original noticing to exist without deciding whether it was acceptable?

What you're noticing.

EXPLORATION 22.2: The Plausibility Filter
Can It Be Real?

Objective

To notice when plausibility replaces direct registration of information.

Setup

Use during ordinary noticing (while observing a room, a conversation, timing between events, or shifts in mood or atmosphere).

Steps

1. Notice something subtle registering. (It may appear as a small shift, impression, or pattern rather than a clear conclusion.)
2. Ask: *What actually registered first?*
3. Stay with the signal itself rather than the explanation.
4. Then ask: *Did my system dismiss it because it lacked clarity, or because it lacked precedent?*
5. Briefly suspend the plausibility check. (Let the perception remain present without deciding whether it is realistic, reasonable, or correct.)
6. Pause without resolving the question.

What to Watch For

⟩ an automatic dismissal of unfamiliar information
⟩ your attention shifting toward explanation rather than observation
⟩ steadiness increasing when plausibility is briefly set aside
⟩ the signal remaining present even without explanation

Reflection

↺ Did the perception fade because it lacked strength, or because it lacked precedent?
↺ What assumption about "how things work" activated first?
↺ Did the dismissal feel analytical, automatic, or neutral rather than emotional?
↺ If no conclusion were required, could the perception remain without strain?
↺ What changes when familiarity is not treated as a requirement for validity?

What you're noticing.

EXPLORATION 22.3: Identity Containment
Who I'm Allowed to Be?

Objective

To notice when identity boundaries limit what can enter your awareness.

Setup

Choose a moment when a perception felt restricted, self-conscious, or edited.

Steps

1. Ask: *Who would I have to be for this perception to feel acceptable?*
2. Notice what identity frame becomes active. For example:
   → professional role
   → social persona
   → group affiliation
   → personal self-image
   → expectations about how "someone like me" should think or respond
3. Notice how your attention reorganizes under that identity.
   → Does your awareness narrow toward what fits the role?
   → Does certain information feel inappropriate to acknowledge?
4. Let the identity frame loosen temporarily.
5. Return your attention to direct experience without deciding what the perception means.

What to Watch For

⟩ a slight expansion when identity loosens
⟩ reduced internal monitoring
⟩ greater steadiness in the original perception
⟩ your awareness expanding without threatening coherences

Reflection

↺ What identity was most active in this moment?
↺ Did the information narrow to remain consistent with that identity?
↺ What would be at risk if this perception were allowed without explanation?
↺ When the role loosened, what changed first?
↺ What remains when no particular identity needs to be maintained?

What you're noticing.

35

EXPLORATION 22.4: The Cultural Echo
Ambient Tone & Misattribution

Objective

To distinguish between your personal registration and ambient social tone.

Setup

Use this exploration in a public space, workplace, media environment, or group setting.

Steps

1. Notice the dominant tone of the environment. (Pay attention to pace, urgency, emotional mood, or collective tension.)
2. Ask: *Is this originating in me, or am I registering the atmosphere around me?*
3. Ground briefly and bring your attention to your breath, posture, and physical connection with your surroundings.
4. Reassess your internal state.
5. Notice what remains when the environmental tone is recognized as context rather than identity.

What to Watch For

⟩ a clearer separation between self and atmosphere
⟩ intensity reducing when context is recognized
⟩ steadiness returning as differentiation increases
⟩ a more defined internal reference point

Reflection

↺ What aspects of what you felt were clearly yours?
↺ What seemed to belong to the environment or group rather than to you?
↺ Did naming the context change your internal state without effort?
↺ How did grounding affect the intensity of what you noticed?
↺ Was there a difference between emotional tone and actual information?
↺ How does recognizing context as context change how you move through similar spaces?

What you're noticing.

EXPLORATION 22.5: Taboo Suspension
The One-Minute Version

Objective

To notice how internalized taboos quietly limit attention.

Temporary Suspension

Rather than pushing against a taboo, briefly allow the possibility that noticing does not require endorsement, explanation, or action. Let the information register without deciding whether it is meaningful, legitimate, or useful.

Setup

Choose one internal rule for a minute:

1. "This can't be real."
2. "I shouldn't notice this."
3. "That's not rational."
4. "I shouldn't trust this."

Steps

1. Hold the rule in your mind.
2. Say silently: *For one minute, this rule can rest.*
3. Notice what registers differently when the rule is not applied.
4. After a minute, allow the rule to return naturally.

What to Watch For

> softening rather than excitement
> increased clarity without effort
> absence of pressure to explain or conclude
> what you perceive remaining steady without endorsement

Reflection

↺ What shifted when the rule was allowed to rest, even briefly?
↺ Did anything new appear, or did something simply become easier to notice?
↺ How did your body respond during the suspension: soften, steady, or remain unchanged?

↺ Did the absence of the rule feel neutral, relieving, or unfamiliar?
↺ When the rule returned, did your awareness contract in a noticeable way?
↺ What does this suggest about how taboos shape attention rather than truth?

What you're noticing.

Integration Practice 22
Maintaining Awareness Without Social Compression

This practice is not about removing social or cultural influence.

It is about staying oriented while influence is present.

Once or twice a day, or after a socially dense interaction:

1. Pause briefly. Do not review or analyze what happened.
2. Ask: *Did anything register that I dismissed before I could evaluate it?*
3. Scan for the five filters without judgment:
   → Was I concerned about how this would look? (Social Permission)
   → Did familiarity override my clarity? (Plausibility)
   → Did my identity need to stay intact? (Identity Containment)
   → Was I absorbing shared atmosphere? (Cultural Echo)
   → Did my attention turn away automatically? (Taboo Constraint)
4. Choose one filter only. Do not correct it. Just acknowledge its presence.
5. Ground:
   → Feel your feet.
   → Notice your breath.
   → Re-establish your baseline orientation.
6. Let what you become aware of remain unresolved.

This practice restores perceptual range without destabilizing social coherence.

It allows what you are aware of to register fully while remaining human, relational, and grounded.

Closing Thought

Cultural and social filters do not create false perception.

They restrict what is allowed into view.

Most limits on awareness are not imposed through force or fear, but through quiet agreements about what is reasonable to notice and what is better left unattended.

Recognizing these filters does not require rebellion, explanation, or withdrawal. It requires orientation.

When what you are aware of is allowed to register privately (before judgment, before plausibility, before identity) your organismic intelligence regains resolution without losing perceptual coherence.

⟩   You do not need to step outside culture to remain perceptive.
⟩   You only need to notice when your range is being reduced.

From here, what registers becomes neither oppositional nor naïve.

It becomes usable.

23 I The Limits of Awareness
When Perception Is Shaped, Not Missing

Opening Invitation

The previous chapter explored how cultural conditioning shapes perception within your system.

This chapter looks at what happens when those same dynamics operate at scale.

Up to this point, the focus has been on how information registers, stabilizes, differentiates, and integrates within your system.

Here, that inquiry moves outward to examine how perceptual mechanisms shape environments, relationships, groups, and historical momentum.

This is explored not as theory or critique, but as lived dynamics.

This chapter delves into how your awareness can narrow not because information is absent, but because perception itself is shaped, filtered, and regulated (sometimes unobtrusively, sometimes collectively) until entire regions of experience no longer register at all.

When Awareness Is Limited, Not Absent

It is common to assume that confusion, rigidity, or harm arise from ignorance, from a lack of knowledge, education, or aptitude.

But perception does not fail only when information is missing.

It also fails when awareness itself is constrained.

A person can be highly informed and still profoundly limited in what they are able to notice, question, or register as relevant. In such cases, the issue is not ignorance, but the narrowing of the perceptual bandwidth: what is allowed to come into awareness at all.

Much of what we call order(social, psychological, cultural, even perceptual) is maintained not by understanding, but by limited awareness.

This limitation does not require force, coercion, or deception. It is usually far subtler than that.

It often emerges through:

> unexamined norms
> inherited frames of reference
> social pressure to perceive "appropriately"
> shared assumptions about what is official, acceptable, or real

These constraints rarely announce themselves as constraints.

They are absorbed early, reinforced often, and eventually experienced as *common sense*.

Over time, your system adapts to them automatically.

One of the more counterintuitive aspects of awareness is this: what is excluded from awareness does not feel missing.

When a range of what can be perceived is never activated (or is actively discouraged) it does not register as an absence. It simply does not appear on the internal map of what seems possible, relevant, or thinkable.

Because of this, limited awareness often presents as certainty rather than confusion.

The more stable a system of limits is, the less likely it is to be questioned.

Official & Unofficial Awareness

Some forms of awareness are discouraged not because they are false, but because they are unofficial.

Official awareness consists of what a given environment (family, profession, culture, institution) implicitly agrees is valid, relevant, and speakable. It defines what is reasonable to notice, what counts as evidence, and what kinds of perception are supported rather than questioned.

Unofficial awareness falls outside those agreements. It may be accurate, subtle, or even useful, but it does not fit the sanctioned frame.

As discussed in Chapter 22, societal filters do not merely shape opinions or beliefs; they shape what registers in awareness in the first place.

They operate prior to interpretation, influencing which signals are amplified, which are muted, and which never fully form as perceptions at all.

A simple example can be seen in many workplaces.

During a meeting, a project may be presented as successful and moving smoothly. The official tone is confident and optimistic.

Yet several people in the room may privately notice something else:

> hesitation in the presenter's voice
> incomplete answers to practical questions
> tension between team members
> small inconsistencies in the timeline

Individually, these signals register. But because the official narrative of the meeting is that the project is "on track," those perceptions often remain unofficial.

No one names them directly. Questions soften. Attention shifts.

The signals are present, but they do not organize into shared awareness

Because of this, unofficial awareness carries real risk:

> social friction
> loss of belonging
> being seen as disruptive, strange, or unreliable

These risks do not need to be enforced explicitly. Over time, they are internalized.

As a result, many people unconsciously regulate what they allow themselves to notice. This regulation rarely feels like suppression.

More often, it feels like being appropriate, realistic, or well-adjusted.

What is registered narrows not through force, but through self-adjustment.

This is not a conspiracy.

It is a perceptual economy.

Pause. Check resonance.

When Information Disappears Without Being Absent

There are moments in experience when something should be obvious yet does not register.

> Not because it is hidden.
> Not because it is unknown.

But because it cannot pass through the way awareness is currently organized.

In such moments, information does not arrive as confusion or uncertainty; it simply vanishes.

Questions fall flat. Contradictions slide past unnoticed. Signals that normally prompt curiosity, concern, or reflection fail to register at all.

This is not ignorance in the usual sense.

It is a perceptual phenomenon.

When filtering becomes complete, what you are aware of does not merely narrow.

It collapses.

The perception does not stabilize. What disappears is not the signal itself.

It is the ability of awareness to organize that signal into something recognizable.

History offers many examples of this effect.

When the first reports of meteorites falling from the sky reached European scientific institutions in the eighteenth century, they were widely dismissed. Stones could not fall from the sky, the reasoning went, because there were no stones in the sky. Witnesses were assumed to be mistaken, superstitious, or exaggerating.

The stones themselves were often present. The reports were documented. But the information could not organize into awareness within the prevailing framework of plausibility.

Only after repeated observations (and eventually the public fall of a meteorite in L'Aigle, France in 1803) did the scientific community revise its assumptions and recognize what had been occurring all along.

The stones had never been absent. Only the possibility had been filtered out.

Black Holes in Awareness

Not all limitations of what registers are equal.

Some gaps in awareness function like knowledge vacuums. In these cases:

> information is absent
> understanding is incomplete
> the consequences tend to remain largely personal

A person may be misinformed, undereducated, or simply unaware, but new information can often be introduced without resistance. Knowledge vacuums are frustrating, but they are usually permeable.

Other limitations function very differently. They do not lack information. They absorb awareness.

These are black holes in awareness: regions where perception cannot reach beyond, not because nothing is there, but because incoming information is filtered, neutralized, or rendered irrelevant before it can register as meaningful.

Attention approaches the boundary and simply disappears.

As Ingo noted, this distinction is not about brainpower or education. It is about how reality is structured within one's system itself.

Knowledge vacuums arise where information has not yet been integrated.

Black holes arise where what can be perceived is actively prevented from integrating at all... usually because it cannot be reconciled with an existing reality structure.

A simple illustration can appear in academic environments.

A university may take pride in seeing itself as intellectually open, supportive, and attentive to student well-being. That identity becomes part of how the institution understands itself.

Over time, small signals may begin to appear: students quietly describing overwhelming workloads, increases in withdrawal or burnout, faculty noticing rising stress in classrooms.

The information is present. But if the institution's identity depends on the belief that it already provides a balanced and supportive environment, those signals may fail to register as meaningful.

They may be explained away as individual resilience issues, temporary academic pressure, or the normal demands of rigorous study.

The signals are visible, but the pattern never stabilizes into awareness.

Black holes in awareness are not empty. They are dense.

This is what makes black holes in awareness particularly consequential. Unlike knowledge vacuums, their effects rarely remain confined to the individual.

Because they shape action without being visible to reflection, they can influence decisions, systems, and groups, often while remaining entirely invisible to those operating within them.

Importantly, black holes in awareness cannot usually be recognized directly.

Just as an astronomical black hole cannot be seen by light, perceptual black holes are detected only by their effects:

> by what consistently fails to register
> by what cannot be questioned
> by what is repeatedly justified without examination

Pause. Check resonance.

Recognizing Black Holes in Lived Experience

Black holes in awareness are rarely experienced as confusion or uncertainty. More often, they are experienced as clarity.

They can often be recognized by their effects:

> disproportionate certainty
> hostility toward nuance
> emotional reactivity in place of curiosity
> rigid narratives that resist direct experience
> loss of relational attunement

In these moments, data narrows abruptly.

Complexity collapses into a single explanatory frame, and alternative signals (context, tone, contradictory data, lived feedback) fail to register as relevant.

Importantly, these are not signs of evil, pathology, or personal failure.

They are signs of perceptual collapse under pressure.

When an existing reality structure is challenged beyond its tolerance, awareness does not gradually adjust. It contracts.

Attention is pulled toward what preserves coherence, identity, or moral certainty, while anything that threatens that stability is absorbed and neutralized.

This is why black holes in awareness are often accompanied by strong affect. Emotional intensity functions as a stabilizer, locking perception into a narrowed range and discouraging further inquiry.

Curiosity becomes unsafe; certainty becomes protective.

Recognizing this pattern changes how one responds.

Instead of opposition (arguing, correcting, or confronting) it becomes possible to navigate.

Navigation involves maintaining one's own perceptual flexibility while avoiding direct pressure on the collapsed region.

It favors pacing, indirect engagement, and restoring conditions under which curiosity can safely re-emerge.

From this perspective, recognition itself is already a form of active awareness. It allows organismic perception to remain mobile rather than reactive, and interaction to remain relational rather than adversarial.

Ignorance, Power, & Awareness

Seen clearly, the pattern is simple: ignorance preserves order by maintaining narrow bandwidths of awareness.

Within those bandwidths, life feels predictable, roles feel stable, and meaning feels unquestioned.

When those lenses are strained (by contradiction, novelty, or lived experience that no longer fits), power tends to appear.

At the individual level, power does not usually look like domination.

> It looks like certainty hardening.
> It looks like rules replacing discernment.
> It looks like authority replacing orientation.

A simple example can appear in family conversations. A pattern may exist that everyone senses but rarely names, perhaps a recurring tension around finances, expectations, or responsibility. Occasionally someone begins to point toward it.

The response often comes quickly.

> "Let's not make this a big deal."
> "That's just how things are."
> "We're not going to argue about this."

Nothing overtly forceful occurs, yet the conversation closes. The signals that prompted the question remain present, but the space for noticing them disappears.

Awareness does not oppose order; it outgrows the perceptual constraints that made rigid order necessary.

This is why active awareness often feels disruptive. It is not because it seeks chaos, but because it dissolves the need for enforced coherence. What once had to be held in place through control can now be navigated through organismic perception.

Power, in this sense, does not create coherence. It compensates for its absence.

When internal coherence is lost, control steps in. When understanding weakens, enforcement strengthens.

This dynamic can be observed not only in systems, but in everyday interactions: arguments, roles, identities, and even self-talk. Seen this way, the act of being aware does not overthrow structure. It renders brittle structures obsolete by making them unnecessary.

Pause. Check resonance.

EXPLORATION 23.1: Recognizing Perceptual Density
When Awareness Compresses Instead of Expanding

Objective

To notice how your active awareness responds when encountering rigid or collapsed perceptual bandwidths.

Setup

Sit upright or supported and let your breath regulate itself.

Steps

1. Recall a recent interaction, environment, or situation that felt unusually rigid, tense, or closed.
2. Notice:
   → your body's response
   → emotional tone
   → boundary shifts
3. Ask: *Does what I can perceive feel blocked, compressed, or absorbed here?*
4. Return to grounding.

What to Watch For

⟩ a sense of compression, heaviness, or narrowing in your attention
⟩ bodily signals such as pressure, tightening, flattening, or withdrawal
⟩ your emotional tone shifting toward certainty, dullness, or irritation
⟩ reduced curiosity or difficulty holding multiple perspectives
⟩ a feeling that information "goes nowhere" or does not circulate
⟩ an impulse to disengage, harden, or explain prematurely

Reflection

↺ What did your system register before your thoughts intervened?
↺ Where in your body did the sense of compression appear first?
↺ Did the environment feel dense because information was absent, or because it could not circulate?
↺ Did you feel pressure to simplify, agree, withdraw, or explain?
↺ What happened when you allowed the compression to be noticed without trying to resolve it?

EXPLORATION 23.2: Staying Oriented Without Resistance
Maintaining Coherence

Objective

To practice remaining perceptually coherent without trying to change the situation.

Setup

Sit in stillness and allow your breathing to even out on its own.

Steps

1. Bring to mind a context where your perceptual range contracts.
2. Anchor in:
    → breath
    → posture
    → physical sensation
3. Allow what you perceive to remain open without pushing.

What to Watch For

⟩ stabilization in your breath or posture when effort drops
⟩ your boundary returning closer to the body rather than expanding outward
⟩ your awareness becoming quieter rather than clearer or more detailed
⟩ reduced urgency to respond, correct, or interpret
⟩ remaining present without engagement or absorption
⟩ a sense of "standing nearby"

Reflection

↺ What happened when you stopped trying to change the perceptual range?
↺ Did your orientation stabilize on its own?
↺ What shifted first when effort dropped (breath, posture, or attention)?
↺ Did the situation feel different when you remained oriented without engaging it?
↺ What remains when your awareness stays present without needing to act or resolve?

What you're noticing.

59

EXPLORATION 23.3: When Awareness Slips Through
The Moment Something Becomes Visible

Objective

To notice how your system sometimes registers information spontaneously, without effort, intention, or analysis.

Setup

No preparation is required. This exploration takes place within daily life.

Steps

1. Recall a recent moment when you noticed something and thought: "I've been here before, but I never saw that."
2. Do not analyze what was noticed. Instead, attend to:
   → the timing of the recognition
   → your internal state just before it occurred
3. Ask:
   → Was I trying to see this?
   → Was I more relaxed, distracted, or present than usual?
4. Notice what shifted in your system at the moment of recognition:
   → breath
   → posture
   → emotional tone
   → sense of orientation
5. Return to ordinary activity without pursuing the insight.

What to Watch For

〉 recognition arriving without effort
〉 curiosity without urgency
〉 a brief sense of surprise or clarity

Reflection

↺ What allowed this to be seen now?
↺ What was not present when recognition occurred (pressure, certainty, urgency)?
↺ Did your awareness feel wider, quieter, or more ordinary afterward?

Integration Practice 23
Being Aware Without Absorption

At moments throughout your day, notice:

1. Where does your organismic intelligence flow easily?
2. Where does it feel dense, rigid, or absent?
3. Can you remain yourself without forcing clarity?

This is not withdrawal.

It is discernment.

Observations.

Closing Thought

Darkness is not ignorance.

It is managed awareness.

What fails is not your perceptual awareness system, but permission to notice, to linger, to let what you perceive reorganize itself.

Your awareness does not vanish under pressure.

> It narrows.
> It adjusts.
> It waits.

It does not survive in monuments or institutions.

It survives in small moments, when people briefly forget who they are supposed to be and remember how to notice.

What follows is not prescription.

It is orientation.

And orientation, once regained, tends to persist, even when the structures around it remain unchanged.

24 I The Plausibility Factor
When Explanation Shapes What Is Considered Real

Opening Invitation

In Chapter 22, the plausibility filter was introduced as an internal mechanism: the process by which information is compressed when it does not fit existing models of reality.

Chapter 23 explored what happens when perceptual constraints solidify into structural collapse.

Here, plausibility is no longer examined as an individual filter, but as a collective stabilizer.

It is not about how awareness disappears, rather how it survives by changing shape.

When signal encounters structures that cannot tolerate certain forms of knowing, it does not always collapse.

Sometimes, it translates.

Information is not rejected.

It is reframed.

Where the plausibility filter once seemed confined to the individual, it now operates across systems, shaping language, research, explanation, credibility, and institutional response.

The emphasis here is not on whether perceptions are correct or incorrect.

It is on how explanation determines what is allowed to count as real.

When Plausibility Replaces Perception

Most people assume that what is perceivable is limited by absence of data.

But more often, it is limited by plausibility.

Plausibility does not ask whether something registers clearly.

It asks whether it fits.

It determines:

> what explanations feel reasonable
> what interpretations feel safe
> what kinds of knowing are acceptable
> what forms of awareness are permitted to stabilize
> what questions are allowed to form fully

When an experience does not fit the available explanatory frame, one of three things tends to happen:

> It is dismissed.
> It is pathologized.
> It is translated.

Dismissal removes the signal, pathologizing contains it, and translation reshapes it.

Translation is the craftiest. Because translation allows the data to continue... under new language.

The information remains, but its meaning shifts. Its edges soften. Its implications narrow. Its disruptive potential dissolves.

Over time, translation becomes automatic.

The original data is no longer remembered as distinct from its explanation.

Plausibility rarely announces itself as constraint.

> It feels like rationality.
> It feels like realism.
> It feels like intellectual discipline.
> It feels like being well-adjusted.

But plausibility is not neutral.

> It is historically shaped.
> It is socially reinforced.
> It is rewarded in institutions and internalized in identity.

And when plausibility becomes the primary gatekeeper, the information does not disappear.

It is reformatted to fit prevailing assumptions.

Pause. Check resonance.

" "

Even so, it is often an uncomfortable, mind-bending shock to encounter something that challenges established certainty. Because certainty is generally preferred to uncertainty, experiences that introduce ambiguity are often resisted or avoided before they are examined.

— Adapted from Ingo Swann, *Remote Viewing: The Real Story*

Notes.

From Anomaly to Mechanism

Throughout history, experiences that fall outside dominant explanatory frameworks do not always disappear.

More often, they are translated.

In the mid-1970s, U.S. intelligence sought to assess reports that Soviet researchers were investigating what they termed psychotronics.

Psychotronics was a Soviet umbrella term used to describe research into anomalous perception and mind–matter interaction, framed not as mysticism, but as biophysical or electromagnetic processes occurring within living systems.

Rather than treating perception as spiritual agency, it was approached as a potential interaction between biological organisms and measurable interactions.

The question for the United States was not whether such phenomena were philosophically persuasive.

It was whether they were technologically relevant.

Notably, the assessment was not commissioned through a parapsychology foundation or a consciousness research institute. It was assigned to Garrett AiResearch, an aerospace engineering firm known for its work in aviation and defense systems.

The resulting report examined what it termed "Novel Biophysical Information Transfer Mechanisms."

Its language was technical:

> electrostatics
> electromagnetic fields
> signal extraction
> interference
> instrumentation
> low-frequency emissions

Rather than describing anomalous perception in spiritual vocabulary, the report treated it as a possible signal process within biological systems.

The phenomenon did not change.

The explanatory container did.

The phenomenon was reorganized into language compatible with prevailing scientific and defense frameworks.

In that language, it could be evaluated without destabilizing underlying assumptions.

> Mechanism carries credibility in technological cultures.
> Electronic language stabilizes what mystical language destabilizes.
> Signal processing feels investigable.
> Biophysical interaction feels measurable.

Anomalous perception did not need to be believed in order to be studied. It only needed to be modeled.

This was not necessarily deception. It was structural adaptation.

When information cannot survive inside one explanatory frame, it migrates into another.

Plausibility did not eliminate what one can be aware of. It reshaped it so it could remain.

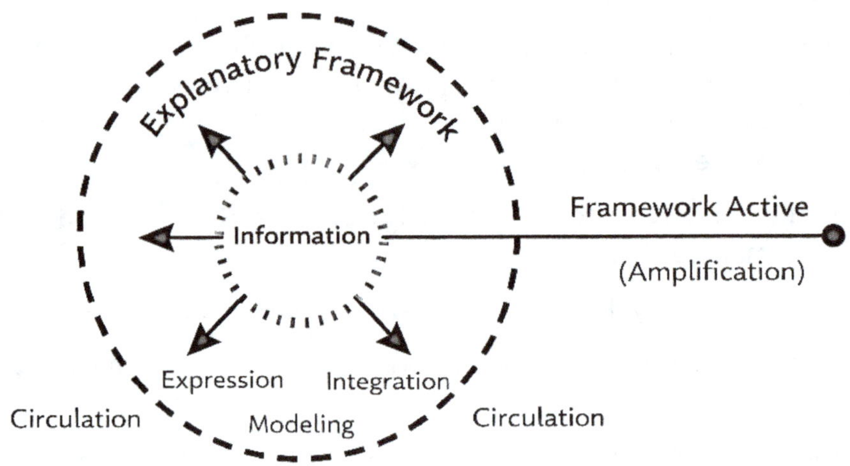

Explanatory Framework
Information
Framework Active
(Amplification)
Expression
Integration
Circulation
Modeling
Circulation

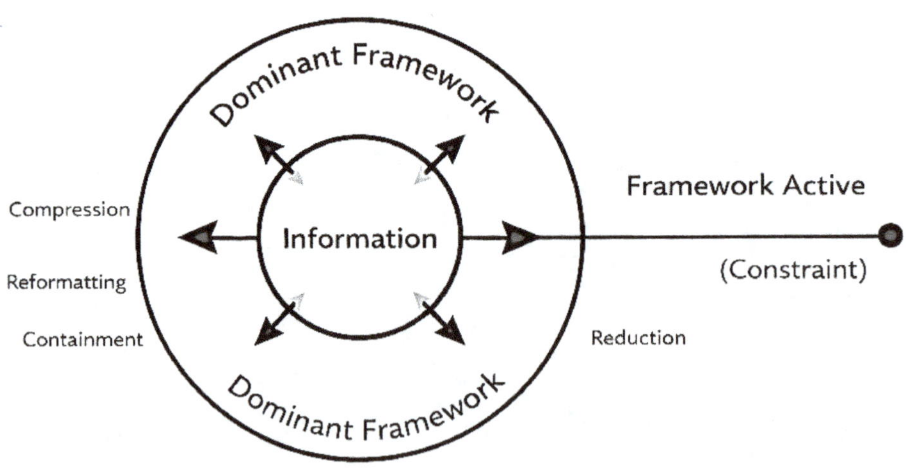

Dominant Framework
Information
Framework Active
(Constraint)
Compression
Reformatting
Containment
Reduction
Dominant Framework

Pause. Check resonance.

Official Explanation & Perceptual Survival

As discussed in Chapter 23, official awareness defines what is speakable.

Plausibility defines what is explainable.

The distinction matters.

A perception framed as mystical may be dismissed.

The same perception framed as statistical signal variation may be funded.

What changes is not necessarily the underlying experience.

It is the explanatory container through which that experience must pass.

Plausibility functions less like a wall and more like a membrane.

> It does not block everything.
> It filters.
> It determines which forms of data are stabilized, which are softened, and which are reorganized before they are allowed to circulate.

This membrane operates at multiple levels:

> personal identity
> professional culture
> scientific consensus
> political climate
> social belonging

When plausibility tightens, signal does not always vanish.

> It adapts.
> It reorganizes itself into terms that can survive.

This reorganization is rarely experienced as compromise.

> The individual believes they are being rational.
> The institution believes it is being responsible.

What is being preserved is not necessarily truth.

It is structural coherence.

Pause. Check resonance.

The Plausibility Filter in Everyday Life

The plausibility factor is not limited to institutions. It operates internally.

Consider:

> dismissing an inferential knowing because it "sounds dramatic"
> translating emotional knowing into productivity language
> reframing discomfort as inefficiency rather than misalignment
> reducing relational tension to miscommunication rather than incompatibility

In each case, data is not absent.

It is converted.

Converted into language that feels safer, more reasonable, more defensible.

A simple version of this happens in everyday conversation.

Someone may notice a subtle discomfort while interacting with a group online. The tone feels exaggerated, the certainty feels forced, or the emotional reaction being encouraged seems disproportionate to the information being discussed.

The signal registers briefly.

But because the conversation is widely affirmed (liked, shared, and repeated) the information is often translated.

Instead of questioning the signal, the person may conclude:

> "I'm probably reading too much into this."
> "This is just how people talk online."

The original data does not disappear.

It is reorganized into a more plausible explanation.

Translation preserves continuity, but it also reshapes meaning.

Over time, this translation becomes automatic. One no longer notices the shift between perception and explanation.

The frame feels self-generated, but it is inherited.

And because it is inherited, it feels natural.

When Explanation Hardens

Plausibility becomes distortion when explanation hardens into exclusivity.

Signs include:

> reflexive skepticism toward certain forms of perception
> automatic elevation of one explanatory model over all others
> discomfort when experience cannot be reduced
> urgency to categorize before fully registering
> identity invested in a particular framework

When explanation hardens, perception narrows. It does this not through collapse, as in Chapter 23, but through compression:

> Everything must fit an existing model.

What cannot be integrated is neutralized through reinterpretation.

Nothing disappears, but nothing destabilizes.

A simple example can appear in ordinary conversation.

Someone may describe a persistent feeling that something in their work or relationship is misaligned. The signal may be understated: fatigue, unease, or a sense that something does not fit.

But if the dominant explanatory frame in the conversation is purely psychological or productivity-based, the response often arrives quickly.

> "You're probably just stressed."
> "Everyone feels that way sometimes."
> "You just need better boundaries."

The original perception is not rejected outright. It is translated into a form that fits the available model.

The signal remains but its meaning has been compressed.

This is subtler than a black hole in awareness.

Black holes absorb.

Hardened explanation converts.

Conversion feels orderly.

But order achieved through over-translation is a quiet form of perceptual reduction.

Pause. Check resonance.

Plausibility & Power

Where perception must translate itself in order to be acceptable, power is already operating.

Power does not always silence awareness.

Often, it reshapes it.

> Institutional power favors explanations that preserve order.
> Social power favors explanations that preserve belonging.
> Psychological power favors explanations that preserve identity.

None of these forces are inherently malicious. They are stabilizing mechanisms.

But stabilization has consequences.

A simple example can appear within a sports team.

During practice or a game, a player may notice that a particular strategy is not working. The opposing team is anticipating it, and the pattern is becoming obvious.

The signal registers clearly.

But if the now faltering strategy comes from a respected coach or team leader, the concern may not be voiced directly.

Instead, it may be translated into a softer form: a question about timing, a suggestion to adjust positioning, or a comment about needing better execution.

The information remains present, but it is reshaped into language that preserves team cohesion and authority.

When explanatory frames harden, they determine not only what is noticed, but what is allowed to remain visible without penalty.

The plausibility factor does not merely influence perception. It regulates which data survives.

Pause. Check resonance.

EXPLORATION 24.1: Noticing Translation in Real Time
When Information Is Reframed Automatically

Objective

To notice when what can be perceived is translated into a more plausible explanation.

Setup

Sit in a stable posture and allow your breathing to find its own rhythm.

Steps

1. Recall a recent experience where you quickly explained something away.
2. Ask:
    - → What did I notice first?
    - → What explanation did I apply?
3. Separate:
    - → signal (raw perception)
    - → applied explanation
4. Notice the difference in tone between the two.

What to Watch For

- ⟩ flattening of experience after explanation
- ⟩ emotional charge decreasing or increasing with framing
- ⟩ shifts in your posture or boundary
- ⟩ impulse to defend the explanation

Reflection

- ↻ What changed between your original perception and your applied explanation?
- ↻ Did the explanation clarify the experience, or reduce it?
- ↻ What was preserved by translating it into something more plausible (stability, identity, coherence)?
- ↻ What was lost in that translation?
- ↻ Did your explanation arise from evidence, or from the need for resolution?
- ↻ If no explanation were required, could the original perception stand on its own?

EXPLORATION 24.2: Holding Before Naming
Letting Experience Organize Before Framing

Objective

To briefly allow information to remain present before translating it into explanation.

Setup

Take a seat and allow your breathing to slow without effort.

Steps

1. Notice something subtle in your present experience. (It may appear as a sensation, tone, atmosphere, or small shift in your attention.)
2. Delay naming it.
   → If a label arises, simply let it pass without following it.
3. Hold the experience as texture rather than explanation.
4. Notice qualities such as movement, density, or emotional tone.
5. Stay grounded in your breath, posture, and physical sensation.

What to Watch For

⟩ discomfort without explanation
⟩ widening of your attention
⟩ increased neutrality
⟩ spontaneous reorganization

Reflection

↺ What shifted when naming was delayed?
↺ Did the experience intensify, diminish, or stabilize without explanation?
↺ Was there pressure to conclude, or could the experience remain open?
↺ Did meaning begin to organize differently when you did not intervene?
↺ What part of you wanted to name it first: habit, discomfort, identity, plausibility?
↺ If you eventually named it, did the label match the texture you first sensed?

What you're noticing.

EXPLORATION 24.3: The Edge of Plausibility
Where Experience Meets Your Explanatory Limits

Objective

To recognize where your own plausibility boundaries sit.

Setup

Sit comfortably and let your breath move naturally.

Steps

1. Notice a type of information you tend to dismiss quickly.
2. Do not adopt it. Simply observe your reaction.
3. Ask:
   - → What feels implausible here?
   - → What would accepting this threaten?
4. Return to grounding.

What to Watch For

⟩ identity tension
⟩ emotional defensiveness
⟩ tightening in your body
⟩ narrative activation

Reflection

↺ Where did the boundary of plausibility appear in your body or posture?
↺ Did the reaction feel protective, dismissive, or analytical?
↺ What structure (identity, role, worldview, stability) would be affected if this were allowed?
↺ Was the response about evidence, or about coherence?
↺ Did the information feel implausible, or simply unfamiliar?
↺ If your boundary softened slightly, what changed first: tension, narrative, or certainty?
↺ Does recognizing the boundary alter how firmly it needs to be held?

Integration Practice 24
Information Before Explanation

Throughout the day, notice the moment when data becomes explanation:

1. When do I move immediately from noticing to explaining what something means?
2. When can I pause briefly and allow the data to remain as it first appeared?
3. What changes when explanation is delayed, even for a few seconds?

This is not abandoning reason.

It is expanding what reason is allowed to consider.

Observations.

Closing Thought

Information rarely disappears outright.

More often, it adapts.

> It changes language.
> It alters form.
> It reshapes itself until it fits the structure it inhabits.

Plausibility is not the enemy of awareness, however, when it hardens, it becomes its boundary.

To recognize the plausibility factor is not to reject explanation. It is to see that explanation is never neutral.

And once seen, your awareness regains mobility.

25 | Geopolitical & Geomagnetic
The Larger Forces in Motion

Opening Invitation

Up to this point in the series, the focus has been on how perception organizes within human systems: the body, emotion, relationship, and the interpretive structures that shape meaning.

In the preceding chapters of this book, you have noticed how:

> cultural assumptions influence what feels reasonable to notice
> plausibility structures shape what explanations are allowed to stabilize
> informational environments amplify some signals while diminishing others

These influences shape perception from within human systems.

But they are not the only conditions within which awareness unfolds.

Awareness also develops within larger environments that influence:

> how information circulates,
> how interpretation stabilizes
> what becomes recognizable as meaningful

Some of these influences are social and informational.

Others arise from the broader planetary conditions within which life itself evolved.

Informational Influences

Social and informational environments shape how meaning circulates and stabilizes, and how certain interpretations gain credibility while others fade from view.

Signals move through networks of attention long before individuals decide what they think about them.

Images circulate → stories repeat → interpretations stabilize.

Over time, what receives repeated attention begins to gather weight within shared awareness.

Planetary Influences

Yet human awareness does not unfold only within social or informational environments.

It unfolds within a planetary environment as well.

The Earth itself generates dynamic conditions that surround every living organism. These include:

> solar radiation
> geomagnetic activity
> gravitational relationships with the Moon
> atmospheric and electromagnetic dynamics

Most of the time these influences remain unnoticed. They form part of the background conditions within which perception occurs.

Biological systems evolved within these rhythms.

Human physiology did not develop apart from the Earth's relationship with the Sun, the Moon, and the surrounding space environment.

Circadian cycles follow the rotation of the planet.

Seasonal changes follow its orbit.

Tidal rhythms reflect the gravitational relationship between Earth and Moon.

Context

From this perspective, perception unfolds within multiple layers of context.

These contexts do not usually block perception outright. More often, they shape the thresholds through which signals organize within awareness.

Some contexts are informational.

Others are social and geopolitical.

Still others are planetary.

The aim here is not to claim that these forces determine perception. It is simply to recognize that awareness never occurs in isolation.

Interpretation unfolds within environments.

Explanation does not simply describe reality.

It determines what is allowed to carry weight as real.

Try to note when you are feeling well and energetic and when not.

Look around you to see whether others are experiencing the same thing.

We often assume these states are purely personal, yet they may reflect broader conditions affecting more than just you.

— Adapted from Ingo Swann, *Psychic Literacy*

Notes.

The Environment of Influence

In recent years, the word influencer has become widely associated with social media personalities whose opinions, preferences, or lifestyles attract large audiences.

Millions of people follow individuals they may never meet.

They watch how they dress, what they eat, where they travel, what they believe, and how they interpret events in the world.

At first glance, this phenomenon can appear unusual: *Why would so many people orient their attention toward someone they do not personally know?*

Yet from the perspective of perception, the mechanism itself is not new. Humans have always been influenced by the attention of others.

> We notice what others notice.
> We evaluate what others evaluate.
> We orient toward signals that appear to carry shared importance.

Influence begins with attention. Where attention gathers, significance begins to form. What has changed in recent years is not the mechanism of influence but its scale and reach.

Digital communication systems allow attention to converge across distance. Signals can circulate rapidly through networks that connect millions of people simultaneously.

Influence no longer depends on physical proximity or shared space. It travels through images, language, stories, and repeated interpretation.

In Book Two, you explored a related phenomenon described as the Invisible Crowd. There, the focus was on how what you perceive changes in the presence of other people.

Shared emotional tone, posture, rhythm, and proximity create subtle shifts in awareness.

You discovered how to recognize this in everyday life:

> walking into a room and sensing its mood
> feeling tension rise during a conversation
> noticing how attention intensifies when several people focus on the same event

In those situations, influence arises through direct relational signals. Bodies, voices, posture, and emotional tone interact in real time.

You detects these signals automatically.

The result is a form of relational amplification: what you are aware of becomes shaped by the presence and attention of others.

The influencer context operates differently. Here, influence travels without physical presence. It moves through symbolic signals rather than direct physiological cues.

Images, statements, opinions, and interpretations circulate through networks where millions of people encounter them individually yet respond collectively.

> Instead of a shared room, there is a shared informational environment.
> Instead of posture and tone, there are images and narratives.
> Instead of immediate interaction, there is repetition and amplification.

The result is still influence, but it operates through a different pathway.

Attention gathers around signals that are widely visible. → Repetition strengthens recognition. → Visibility creates familiarity. → Familiarity often produces credibility.

Over time, signals that circulate frequently begin to feel culturally significant. They become part of the informational atmosphere through which people interpret events.

In this way, influence becomes an environment rather than an interaction. It shapes what becomes noticeable long before individuals decide what they think about it.

Most people experience this process not as influence but as ordinary information.

> News stories appear.
> Images circulate.
> Opinions repeat across multiple sources.
> Gradually, certain interpretations begin to feel obvious or widely accepted.

Yet behind this sense of consensus often lies a pattern of repeated attention. This is the underlying dynamic of influencer context.

Influence, in this sense, is not primarily about persuasion. It is about guiding attention. It determines which signals gather visibility and which remain peripheral.

Pause. Check resonance.

EXPLORATION 25.1: Following Attention

The Influence of Visibility

Objective

To observe how your attention moves in response to signals that are socially amplified or repeatedly encountered.

Setup

Choose a short period of time (5–10 minutes) when you can scroll through a digital information stream such as:

> social media
> news feeds
> video platforms
> recommended content lists

Use whatever platform you normally encounter in everyday life.

Steps

1. Begin by pausing briefly before opening the platform.
2. Ask yourself: *What is my attention drawn toward first?*
3. Open the feed and allow yourself to scroll slowly.
4. Notice which signals immediately attract your attention:
    → images
    → headlines
    → emotionally charged language
    → familiar personalities
    → topics already circulating widely
5. Do not judge or analyze yet. Simply observe.
6. Now pause and ask a second question: *Is my attention drawn to this because of its content, or because I have seen it repeatedly?*
7. Continue scrolling for a few minutes while noticing patterns:
    → which topics appear multiple times
    → which interpretations repeat
    → which signals feel familiar before you fully read them
8. Close the platform.
9. Take a moment to notice your internal state.

What to Watch For

⟩ your attention moving quickly toward familiar signals
⟩ repeated topics appearing across different sources
⟩ emotional language increasing attention intensity
⟩ a sense of recognition before full understanding
⟩ certain interpretations appearing multiple times

Reflection

↺ Which signals captured your attention first?
↺ Were those signals new, or had you encountered them previously?
↺ Did repetition make certain information feel more significant?
↺ Did any signals feel important before you had evaluated them fully?
↺ What changed when you became aware of how your attention was being guided?

What you're noticing.

EXPLORATION 25.2: Unfollowing Attention
Letting Influence Go

Objective

To observe how the significance of a signal changes when your attention is deliberately withdrawn.

Setup

Choose a topic, story, or signal that is currently receiving significant attention in your informational environment.

It might be:

> a trending news story
> a widely shared video or image
> a public controversy
> a frequently repeated headline
> a personality or influencer appearing repeatedly in your feed

The specific topic is not important. What matters is that it is receiving noticeable attention.

Steps

1. Briefly notice your current level of awareness about this signal.
2. Ask yourself: *How often have I encountered this topic recently?*
3. For the next 24 hours, deliberately withdraw your attention from this signal. This means:
    → do not click related stories
    → do not watch related videos
    → do not follow comment threads
    → do not search for updates
4. If the signal appears naturally (for example in a headline or feed), simply acknowledge it and continue scrolling without engaging.
5. After the observation period, pause and reflect.

What to Watch For

> how frequently the signal appears without you seeking it
> whether your curiosity increases or fades

⟩ whether the topic begins to feel less urgent
⟩ whether your emotional intensity shifts when your attention drops
⟩ whether other signals become more noticeable

Reflection

↺ Did the signal feel less significant when your attention was withdrawn?
↺ Did your curiosity increase or diminish over time?
↺ Did other topics or signals become more visible once attention shifted?
↺ Did the emotional tone associated with the topic change?

What you're noticing.

 **Perception as a Strategic Domain**

The dynamics of influence become even clearer when we examine how perception can be shaped below the level of conscious attention.

Long before the rise of digital media, researchers and advertisers became interested in whether perception could be influenced by signals that operated below conscious awareness.

The idea that messages could shape behavior without being consciously noticed captured public imagination in the mid-twentieth century.

One of the most widely discussed episodes occurred in 1957, when marketing researcher James Vicary claimed to have inserted brief visual messages into a movie theater presentation.

The messages reportedly flashed phrases for only a fraction of a second during a film such as:

"Drink Coca-Cola"

and

"Eat Popcorn"

Vicary claimed that these flashes increased concession sales.

The story spread rapidly and became one of the earliest examples of what came to be called subliminal advertising.

Public reaction was immediate.

Many people worried that advertising might secretly manipulate consumer behavior without awareness.

Governments and regulatory bodies soon investigated the claims.

Later, Vicary admitted that his original experiment had been exaggerated and that the results could not be reliably reproduced.

Although the dramatic claims proved questionable, the controversy sparked decades of research into subliminal perception.

Psychologists began investigating whether signals presented below conscious awareness could still influence perception.

Laboratory studies showed that very brief images or words could sometimes affect recognition speed, emotional tone, or preference when participants were later asked to evaluate related material.

These effects were generally small and short-lived, but they demonstrated an important principle:

Your system processes far more information than what you are aware of.

Modern research describes this process using terms such as:

> implicit processing
> priming
> non-conscious perception

In marketing research, priming refers to the way exposure to a stimulus can subtly influence later judgments or decisions.

For example, exposure to certain images or concepts may slightly increase the likelihood that related products or ideas feel familiar or appealing.

These influences are not commands.

They do not override judgment or free choice.

Instead, they bias attention and interpretation slightly.

When repeated across large populations and communication systems, even small perceptual biases can influence what becomes widely noticed or culturally significant.

This is where subliminal influence intersects with the broader informational environments.

Influence does not usually appear as hidden commands.

More often it emerges through subtle signals that shape attention before deliberate evaluation begins.

Framing language, emotional tone, repeated imagery, and narrative emphasis can all guide perception in ways that operate beneath immediate awareness.

These dynamics do not eliminate individual judgment.

But they do illustrate how perception unfolds within environments where signals are continuously shaping what feels familiar, important, or meaningful.

Understanding this history provides context for the observations that follow.

The purpose is not to suggest hidden control, but to recognize how influence can operate through the structure of communication itself.

In a lecture delivered in 1977 titled "Psychic Warfare", Ingo described similar dynamics while discussing emerging research in perception and behavioral influence.

He noted that modern psychology had already begun exploring techniques designed to influence perception below conscious awareness, writing:

"Since that time, however, perceptual psychology and psychological behaviorism, we now have the refined techniques known as subliminal persuasion, behavioral modification and various forms of covert mind control."

Ingo suggested that such influences did not necessarily operate through obvious persuasion, but through signals that could remain latent within perception and later shape behavior.

As he observed:

"Studies into subliminal effects show that material planted today can be called forth at some later date to influence behavior—like a mental time bomb."

He also noted that everyday communication environments were already saturated with persuasive signals:

"Thus, we all are being bombarded daily with psychic subliminal content, urging us to buy more, drink more, buy this or that soap, and so forth."

Ingo's remarks were not a claim that people could be secretly controlled. Rather, he was pointing toward a broader observation:

When attention is repeatedly guided toward certain signals, those signals begin to shape the informational environment in which perception occurs.

Over time, interpretation tends to stabilize around what receives the most visibility.

In this *sense*, influence does not begin with belief.

It begins with what enters awareness first.

Pause. Check resonance.

EXPLORATION 25.3: Noticing Suggestion
Signals That Guide

Objective

To observe how suggestion can appear within communication before interpretation fully forms.

Setup

Choose a short piece of media that you encounter naturally in everyday life. It might be:

> an advertisement
> a news headline
> a promotional video
> a political message
> a social media post

The content itself is not important. What matters is noticing how it presents its message.

Steps

1. Begin by observing the material once in a relaxed way, just as you normally would.
2. Notice your initial reaction. Allow the reaction to arise naturally. Do you feel:
   → curiosity
   → agreement
   → skepticism
   → emotional engagement
3. Now return to the message and observe it a second time. This time, focus on how the message is delivered rather than what it says. Look for elements such as:
   → emotional language
   → repetition of certain words or images
   → visual emphasis
   → suggestions of urgency or importance
   → associations with status, fear, belonging, or desire
4. Ask yourself: *What is this message inviting my attention to notice first?*
5. Finally, pause and separate the signal from the suggestion.

6. Ask: *What remains if I remove the emotional framing or persuasive cues?*

What to Watch For

> images that evoke emotional responses before information appears
> language that frames interpretation early
> repetition that increases familiarity
> associations that link a product or idea to identity or belonging
> suggestions that imply what the viewer should feel

Reflection

↺ Did the message contain signals that shaped interpretation before the facts were clear?
↺ Did the emotional tone guide your reaction?
↺ Did repetition or imagery influence what felt important?
↺ What changed when you noticed the persuasive structure of the message?

What you're noticing.

EXPLORATION 25.4: The Repetition Effect

The Pull of Significance & Believability

Objective

To observe how repetition influences the *sense* of familiarity and credibility within perception.

Setup

Choose a topic that has appeared repeatedly in your informational environment over the past few days.

It might be:

> a widely shared news story
> a political narrative
> a trending social media topic
> a public controversy
> a frequently repeated advertisement or slogan

The topic itself is not the focus. The focus is the pattern of repetition.

Steps

1. Pause and briefly recall how many times you have encountered this topic recently.
2. Ask yourself: *Where have I seen or heard this message?*
3. Examples might include:
   → headlines
   → social media posts
   → videos
   → conversations
   → commentary
4. Now consider your current impression of the topic. Does it feel:
   → important
   → familiar
   → widely accepted
   → emotionally charged
5. Simply notice the impression.
6. Next, ask a different question: *Would this topic feel as significant if I had encountered it only once?*

7. Observe how familiarity may influence your perception of importance.
8. Finally, focus on the informational environment without the repetition.
9. Ask: *What remains if the repetition is removed?*

What to Watch For

> topics that feel familiar before they are fully understood
> ideas that seem widely accepted because they appear frequently
> emotional reactions that strengthen with repeated exposure
> signals that feel urgent simply because they are encountered often

Reflection

↺ Did repetition increase the sense that the topic was important?
↺ Did familiarity make the message feel more credible?
↺ Would the topic feel different if it appeared only once?
↺ What happens when you become aware of the role repetition plays in shaping your attention?

What you're noticing.

Planetary Context

Solar and Geomagnetic Conditions

Human awareness does not unfold only within psychological or informational environments.

It also unfolds within planetary environments.

The Earth itself generates dynamic conditions that surround every living organism. These include:

> gravitational forces
> atmospheric dynamics
> solar radiation
> geomagnetic activity

Most of the time these influences remain unnoticed.

They form part of the background conditions within which perception occurs.

Yet biological systems evolved within planetary rhythms created by the Earth's relationship to the Sun, Moon, and surrounding space environment.

Day and night regulate circadian rhythms.

Seasonal cycles influence migration, reproduction, and behavior across countless species.

Tidal patterns shape coastal ecosystems and biological timing systems in marine life.

Human physiology is not separate from these rhythms.

It developed within them.

For much of history, civilizations tracked celestial cycles closely.

Ancient agricultural societies observed lunar phases, seasonal solar movements, and planetary alignments in order to coordinate planting, travel, and ritual life.

These observations were not framed in scientific language, but they reflected a recognition that human activity unfolded within a larger celestial environment.

The Sun and the Earth's Magnetic Environment

During the nineteenth century, scientific instruments began measuring aspects of this environment more precisely.

Researchers studying geomagnetism discovered that the Earth's magnetic field was not constant. It fluctuated in response to activity on the Sun.

Solar eruptions release bursts of charged particles and plasma that travel outward through space.

When these solar emissions reach Earth, they interact with the planet's magnetic field and upper atmosphere.

These interactions produce what scientists now call *space weather*.

Solar flares and coronal mass ejections can disturb the Earth's magnetosphere, altering electromagnetic conditions throughout the atmosphere and near-Earth space.

Strong solar storms can disrupt telegraph systems, radio communication, satellite networks, and electrical infrastructure.

One of the earliest documented examples occurred in 1859, during what is now known as the Carrington Event, when a powerful solar storm produced visible auroras across much of the globe and temporarily disabled telegraph networks.

For much of the twentieth century, however, scientists assumed that these electromagnetic disturbances were far too small to influence biological organisms.

Solar activity was treated primarily as an astrophysical phenomenon rather than a biological context.

Early Research into Solar Cycles and Life

By the early twentieth century, some researchers began exploring whether solar activity might correlate with patterns in biological or social behavior.

The Russian scientist Alexander Chizhevsky examined historical records and proposed that periods of increased solar activity sometimes coincided with heightened human social activity.

His work was controversial and remains debated, yet it reflected a growing curiosity about whether solar cycles might influence complex biological systems.

Later investigations shifted toward measurable physiological effects and the study of electromagnetic environments surrounding living organisms.

Research in what became known as geomagnetobiology explored how biological systems might respond to subtle variations in geomagnetic conditions.

Two Soviet researchers played notable roles in this area.

The physicist A. S. Presman, author of *Electromagnetic Fields and Life*, studied how weak electromagnetic fields interact with biological processes.

Another scientist, A. P. Dubrov, published *The Geomagnetic Field and Life*, presenting evidence suggesting possible relationships between geomagnetic activity and biological systems.

These studies proposed that organisms might exist within a larger electromagnetic environment shaped by the interaction between the Earth and the Sun.

Solar Activity and Perceptual Research

In the late 1970s, Ingo began exploring similar questions while examining patterns in perceptual research.

During remote viewing and perception experiments, he noticed that certain days seemed consistently less reliable than others. Performance appeared to fluctuate in ways that were difficult to explain through ordinary experimental variables.

Curious about these irregularities, Ingo and his assistant began making informal comparisons between experimental performance and reports of solar activity.

Although the correlations were preliminary, they suggested that periods of increased solar disturbance sometimes coincided with what he described as "off days" in perceptual performance.

Ingo proposed a research program to examine possible relationships between solar activity and perceptual functioning.

At the time, however, the proposal was rejected.

The prevailing scientific view held that the Sun's electromagnetic influence on Earth was far too weak to affect living organisms.

Undeterred, Ingo continued exploring the idea independently.

When he encountered Soviet research on electromagnetic effects in biological systems, he began to suspect that the invisible environment surrounding Earth might be more significant than previously assumed.

Later researchers, including physicist Dr. Michael Persinger, examined large datasets of perceptual experiments and compared their results with solar and geomagnetic activity levels.

Some analyses suggested that quieter geomagnetic conditions might correspond with more consistent perceptual performance, while disturbed periods appeared to correlate with greater variability.

These findings remain debated and far from conclusive.

Pause. Check resonance.

A Dynamic Planetary Environment

What these investigations helped reveal, however, is that the electromagnetic environment surrounding Earth is not static.

Solar cycles, geomagnetic fluctuations, and atmospheric electrical changes continuously reshape the physical conditions in which biological systems function.

From this perspective, human awareness unfolds within multiple overlapping contexts.

Informational environments shape the signals we encounter in culture and communication.

Planetary environments shape the physical conditions within which biological systems operate.

Neither determines perception on its own.

But together they form part of the broader background within which your system functions.

Recognizing this broader context does not require firm conclusions about cause and effect.

It simply broadens the view.

Human awareness unfolds not only within social and informational systems.

It also unfolds within a living planetary system shaped by the Sun itself.

EXPLORATION 25.5: Solar Flares

In the Sun's Glare

Objective

To become aware of solar flare activity as part of the larger environmental context within which life on Earth unfolds.

Setup

Solar flares are sudden bursts of energy released from the surface of the Sun.

When these eruptions occur, they emit radiation and charged particles that travel outward through space.

Some of this energy eventually interacts with the Earth's upper atmosphere and magnetic field.

Scientific organizations monitor solar flares continuously and classify them according to their intensity:

> A-class (very small)
> B-class
> C-class
> M-class (moderate)
> X-class (strong)

You can check current solar flare activity through publicly available space-weather reports. For this exploration, you only need to notice whether solar flare activity is quiet, moderate, or active.

Steps

1. Choose a period of several days.
2. Each day, briefly check a space-weather report to see whether any solar flares have occurred.
3. Write down the date and the flare classification if one is reported.
4. At the same time, pause and notice your own internal state.
5. Observe simple qualities such as:
    → clarity of attention
    → energy levels
    → sleep quality
    → emotional tone

6. Avoid drawing conclusions during the observation period.
7. After several days, review your notes and simply observe what you recorded.

What to Watch For

⟩ days when solar flare activity is reported
⟩ days when solar conditions appear quiet
⟩ variations in your clarity, focus, or mood
⟩ changes in your sleep or restfulness

Reflection

↺ Did observing solar activity change how you think about environmental context?

↺ Did any patterns appear between solar flare reports and your own experience?

↺ What happens when you consider perception as unfolding within a planetary system rather than only within personal or social conditions?

What you're noticing.

EXPLORATION 25.6: Geomagnetic Conditions

The Earth's Magnetic Response

Objective

To become aware of fluctuations in the Earth's magnetic environment and recognize them as part of the planetary context within which biological systems function.

Setup

When solar particles reach the Earth, they interact with the planet's magnetic field. These interactions can produce disturbances known as geomagnetic storms.

Scientists monitor geomagnetic activity continuously using simple indices that describe how stable or disturbed the Earth's magnetic field is at any given time.

One commonly used measure is the K-index, which describes geomagnetic activity on a scale from quiet to storm conditions.

You do not need to understand the technical details. For this exploration, simply note whether geomagnetic conditions are reported as:

> quiet
> unsettled
> active
> geomagnetic storm conditions.

Steps

1. Choose a period of several days.
2. Each day, check a space-weather or geomagnetic activity report.
3. Write down the general description of geomagnetic conditions for that day.
4. At the same time, briefly notice your own internal state. Observe simple qualities such as your:
    → mental clarity
    → steadiness of attention
    → emotional tone
    → sleep or restfulness
5. Avoid trying to interpret the information during the observation period.
6. After several days, review your notes and simply observe what you recorded.

What to Watch For

> days when geomagnetic activity is quiet
> days when geomagnetic disturbances are reported
> variations in attention or mental clarity
> changes in sleep patterns or energy levels
> any shifts in how you interpret fluctuations in your own state

Reflection

↺ Did observing geomagnetic conditions change how you think about environmental context?

↺ Did any patterns appear between geomagnetic activity and your own experience?

↺ How does it feel to consider awareness as unfolding within both informational and planetary environments?

What you're noticing.

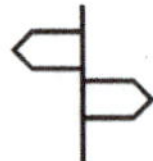

Lunar Cycles and Human Experience

Alongside solar activity and geomagnetic fluctuations, another celestial rhythm has long attracted human attention: the cycle of the Moon.

The Moon completes a visible cycle roughly every twenty-nine and a half days.

During this cycle it moves through familiar phases:

> new moon
> waxing crescent
> first quarter
> waxing gibbous
> full moon
> waning phases returning again to new

For thousands of years, human cultures have tracked these phases carefully.

Lunar calendars were used to organize agricultural activity, religious observances, navigation, and seasonal transitions.

Even the word month shares its linguistic roots with moon, reflecting how deeply lunar cycles were woven into early timekeeping systems.

One of the most widely discussed observations associated with lunar cycles is the so-called full-moon effect.

Across many cultures, folklore has suggested that unusual events, emotional intensity, or changes in human behavior may occur more frequently around the full moon.

These stories appear in traditions around the world and have persisted for centuries.

In modern times, researchers have attempted to evaluate these claims scientifically.

Some studies have examined whether full moons correlate with increases in hospital admissions, crime reports, psychiatric emergencies, or unusual behavior.

The results have been mixed.

Many large studies have found little consistent evidence that the full moon directly causes dramatic changes in behavior.

Pause. Check resonance.

Lunar Phases

Other research has suggested that lunar phases may subtly influence biological rhythms, particularly those related to sleep.

For example, some sleep studies have reported that participants may experience slightly shorter sleep duration or altered sleep cycles near the full moon.

One possible explanation involves light exposure.

Before the widespread use of artificial lighting, the full moon would have been the brightest natural nighttime light source available.

In preindustrial societies this additional illumination may have extended evening activity and subtly shifted sleep patterns.

Another factor involves gravitational forces.

The Moon's gravitational influence drives the Earth's ocean tides.

Many marine species coordinate reproductive and feeding cycles with lunar phases, demonstrating that biological systems can synchronize with lunar rhythms under certain conditions.

Whether similar synchronization occurs within human systems remains an open question.

What is clear is that human perception evolved within a planetary environment shaped by recurring celestial cycles.

Solar activity, geomagnetic fluctuations, seasonal changes, and lunar phases all contribute to the dynamic conditions surrounding life on Earth. Most people rarely consider these influences directly.

Yet they form part of the larger environmental context within which biological systems function.

Recognizing this context does not require assuming that celestial events determine human behavior. Rather, it invites a broader awareness of the rhythms within which perception unfolds.

Just as informational environments shape what we notice in culture and conversation, planetary cycles shape the physical conditions in which awareness operates.

The Moon, like the Sun, is one of the oldest clocks humanity has ever observed.

Pause. Check resonance.

EXPLORATION 25.7: The Moon in Phases
The Lunar Rhythm

Objective

To become aware of lunar phases as part of the recurring celestial rhythms within which life on Earth unfolds.

Setup

The Moon completes a visible cycle approximately every twenty-nine and a half days.

During this cycle it passes through familiar phases:

> new moon
> waxing crescent
> first quarter
> waxing gibbous
> full moon
> waning gibbous
> last quarter
> waning crescent

These phases can be easily observed in the night sky or checked through any lunar calendas.

Steps

1. Choose a period of several days within a single lunar phase.
2. Each evening, briefly note the Moon's current phase.
3. If possible, spend a few moments simply observing the Moon directly.
4. At the same time, notice your own internal state. Observe qualities such as your:
    → emotional tone
    → clarity of attention
    → sleep patterns
    → energy levels
5. Continue this observation across several nights.
6. At the end of the observation period, review your notes and simply notice what you recorded.

What to Watch For

> awareness of the Moon's changing appearance
> shifts in your nighttime environment and illumination
> variations in your sleep patterns or restfulness
> changes in your attention or mood

Reflection

↺ Did observing lunar phases change how you think about environmental cycles?

↺ Did noticing the Moon's presence affect how you experienced the evening environment?

↺ What happens when your organismic intelligence is considered within the rhythm of celestial cycles?

What you're noticing.

Integration Practice 25
The Pull of Influence

At several points during the day, pause briefly and notice something in your environment. It might be:

> a headline or message
> a conversation
> an image or social signal
> a change in mood or attention
> a shift in energy or clarity

Simply notice the moment when perception first appears. Then ask yourself:

1. When do I move immediately from noticing to explaining what something means?
2. Can I pause briefly and allow the perception to remain as it first appeared?
3. What changes when explanation is delayed, even for a few seconds?
4. What additional information becomes visible when interpretation is not immediate?

Observations.

Closing Thought

Recognizing influential contexts does not require skepticism or opposition.

It simply restores awareness of the environments within which your perception unfolds.

Informational systems guide attention.

Social dynamics amplify certain signals.

Planetary conditions quietly shape the biological systems through which awareness operates.

Most of the time these influences remain invisible.

Yet they form the background through which perception moves.

When this background becomes visible, your attention becomes more deliberate.

Signals can be noticed without immediately inheriting the interpretations that accompany them.

Your system becomes capable of distinguishing between the signal itself and the pathways through which attention arrived at it.

Perception remains personal, but it is no longer mistaken for something that occurs in isolation.

It is understood as part of a much larger system of contexts within which what is already there functions.

CODA

REORGANIZING THE MAP OF REALITY

Opening Invitation

Throughout this book, you have explored how perception is shaped long before interpretation begins.

You have seen how attention assigns significance, how plausibility frames what feels reasonable to notice, and how shared structures quietly shape the boundaries of awareness.

Beneath these observations lies a deeper recognition.

What we experience as reality is not the world itself, but the portion of the world our perceptual awareness systems are organized to receive.

This realization raises a further question:

> What happens when information is no longer confined by the assumptions that once organized it?
> What happens when the map through which reality is received begins to reorganize?

This final reflection considers that shift: not as philosophy, and not as technique, but as a structural change in how reality appears.

It reflects one of Ingo's central insights:

> Humans do not experience reality directly.
> They experience the version of reality their perceptual map is organized to receive.

And that map can grow.

Your Reality Is a Map, Not the World Itself

Most people assume perception is complete: *I see what's there. I feel what's real.* Ingo argued the opposite.

What we call reality is the portion of the world our perceptual awareness system is able to register.

This "reality box" is not a flaw. It is a functional structure shaped by:

> childhood conditioning
> cultural assumptions
> emotional patterning
> symbolic associations
> habits of attention

⟩   sensitivities and blind spots
⟩   personal strengths and fears

You do not perceive into emptiness. You perceive through the map already inside you.

Every signal passes through it: filtered, weighted, interpreted.

This is why two people can stand in the same room, sense the same atmosphere, witness the same interaction, and leave with entirely different impressions.

⟩   The difference is not in the signal.
⟩   The difference is in the map.

Understanding this relieves self-doubt and opens the door to genuine perceptual expansion.

You are not "wrong" for perceiving differently.

You are organized differently.

And organization can change.

Closing a Loop Opened at the Beginning

This series began in Book One with a diagram adapted from Ingo's *Secrets of Power, Volume I.*

At the time, you were not asked to understand it. You were not given a framework, a warning, or an interpretation.

You were told only this: Attention gives energy to what it treats as important and withdraws energy from what it treats as unimportant, whether those judgments are accurate or not.

The diagram was meant to wait.

What Has Become Visible Now

Across this book, you have experienced how perception organizes itself when it is allowed to function coherently:

⟩   through selective permeability
⟩   through holding orientation
⟩   through clear differentiation of context

From this vantage point, the diagram from Book One (page 16) can now be seen for what it was always pointing to.

It was never about belief. It was about how significance is assigned before truth is evaluated.

Significance is not inherent in experience. It is conferred by attention. And attention is not neutral.

It is shaped (quietly) by structures of plausibility and permission:

> identity
> plausibility
> social agreement
> cultural norms
> unspoken limits on what is considered "reasonable" to notice

This shaping does not feel like control.

It feels like common *sense*.

Why This Matters Only Now

Earlier in this series, this recognition would have remained abstract.

Now it is experiential.

You have navigated through how:

> what you perceive can remain clear without urgency
> awareness can register without absorbing
> meaning can form without inflation
> orientation can be held even when experience is complex

From this maturity, a further realization becomes unavoidable:

What gains or loses significance in awareness often does so before you decide what you think about it.

This is not manipulation. It is the mechanics of attention.

The Contexts Within Which the Map Forms

Up to this point, the focus has remained primarily on the internal structure of perception: how attention assigns significance, how plausibility filters experience, and how shared assumptions shape what awareness allows.

Yet perception never organizes itself in isolation.

It forms within contexts.

These contexts operate quietly, shaping what signals stabilize and what remains peripheral.

Two broad contexts surround human awareness:

1. Informational Context

The shared narrative environment within which attention circulates.

This includes:

> media systems
> cultural consensus
> dominant explanations
> technological amplification
> social permission

These influences shape which signals are repeated, reinforced, or quietly dismissed.

2. Planetary Context

The physical environment within which biological awareness operates.

Human perception unfolds within a planetary system shaped by:

> solar activity
> geomagnetic conditions
> lunar cycles
> atmospheric dynamics

These influences rarely appear directly in passive awareness, yet they form the environmental background within which biological perception functions.

None of these contexts determine perception completely.

But each influences what becomes easy to notice, difficult to notice, or invisible altogether.

Closing Thought

Living beyond the box does not mean abandoning structure.

It means recognizing that the structures through which reality appears are not fixed.

〉 Attention assigns significance.
〉 Plausibility frames interpretation.
〉 Shared assumptions influence what is allowed to carry weight in perception.

When your perceptual-awareness interchange process stabilizes, these structures become visible.

Reality itself does not change.

But the map through which it is received becomes broader, more flexible, and less constrained by inherited assumptions.

Over time, what receives repeated attention gathers weight.

What gathers weight stabilizes into meaning.

And what stabilizes into meaning gradually becomes what we call reality.

From this vantage point:

〉 What once felt obvious may reveal itself as framing.
〉 What once felt impossible may become perceptible.

Living from this orientation does not require constant effort; it requires steadiness;

The ability to remain aware of both the signal and the frame through which it appears.

From that steadiness, the perceptual process becomes less reactive and more precise.

The world does not become stranger, it becomes larger.

And within that larger context, what you are aware of is no longer confined to the familiar edges of the map.

Instead, you begins to recognize something simple and quietly profound:

Reality has always been larger than the explanations through which we first learned to see it.

SERIES CONCLUSION

Returning to the Original Human Instrument

You have now traveled through the full arc: awakening perception, stabilizing it, and expanding it into a unified system.

At the beginning, nothing was missing from your perceptual awareness system. Your senses were already functioning beneath thought, beneath habit, beneath the noise of modern life. What was missing was recognition.

This series did not give you new abilities.

It helped you recognize capacities that were already present within you.

You navigated through how to:

> feel the space around your body
> sense emotional tone without words
> notice how attention shapes experience
> use boundaries to create clarity
> stabilize what you perceive through coherence
> recognize symbols without mistaking them for facts
> sense time before events arrive
> remain centered while sensing deeply

Along the way, you observed how your system expands and contracts, how interpretation forms, how meaning emerges without force, and how the process reorganizes when allowed to settle.

Gradually, you rediscovered deeper territories (the symbolic, the inferential, the temporal) not as abstractions, but as perceptual ranges grounded humans have always been capable of experiencing.

Ingo spent his life mapping these territories not to elevate perception beyond humanity, but to return it to wholeness. What he pointed toward was never escape. It was integration.

You now have a conscious interface with:

> a body that senses
> an emotional system that communicates
> an intellect that interprets
> attention that interacts
> an awareness that can witness it all

Most people move through life with these systems fragmented or dormant.

You have begun to bring them into alignment.

This matters not because it makes you exceptional, but because it makes you whole.

Human beings are not meant to live only through thought. We are wired to perceive through:

> relationship
> resonance
> attention
> sensitivity
> awareness

These capacities do not isolate you from the world. They connect you to it.

They allow you to:

> feel directly in real time
> recognize your own rhythms
> sense which environments nourish or drain you
> meet others with clarity instead of projection
> respond earlier, more gently, and more wisely

This discovery has been about perceptual literacy: becoming a conscious participant in the subtle dynamics of living.

This is an ongoing conversation between your body, your emotions, your awareness, and the world around you.

You are an instrument. You always were. Now you know how to listen. Now you know how to tune it. Now you know how to play.

Why Humans Have Awareness at All

Awareness did not evolve as a philosophical trait.

It emerged because living systems needed a way to remain oriented within complexity.

Long before language or abstract thought, human survival depended on registering subtle change:

> shifts in mood or intent before conflict
> changes in territory before danger
> patterns in weather, movement, and social dynamics
> internal signals indicating readiness, fatigue, or threat

Awareness is the body's first interface with reality. It detects change before impact.

From a biological perspective, awareness is not separate from the body. It is what a coherent nervous system does when it is not overwhelmed, fragmented, or locked into reflex.

This is why awareness diminishes under chronic stress. A system in survival mode narrows perception to what is immediately actionable. Subtle information drops out, not because it is absent, but because the system cannot afford to receive it.

Awareness, then, is not "higher" perception. It is baseline perception in a regulated system.

The Body as a Coherence Engine

Perception is not a disembodied act. It is a biological event. Your body is not simply receiving information. It is continuously organizing itself in response to it.

Health (perceptual and physiological alike) is not the absence of disturbance. It is the capacity to reorganize coherently.

When attention stabilizes, emotion regulates, and boundaries clarify, system-wide coherence increases. Noise reduces. Signal clarity improves.

Perceptual expansion begins here. Not because new abilities are added, but because your system becomes coherent enough to register finer information without overload.

Thresholds and the Expansion of the Box

Perceptual growth does not occur in a straight line. It occurs at thresholds.

Moments when:

> old assumptions loosen
> control softens
> attention stabilizes
> meaning reorganizes

At these points, your perceptual awareness system briefly leaves its habitual equilibrium. When it settles again, it does so differently.

> This is how biological systems change.
> This is how knowledge embeds.

⟩   This is how the reality box expands.

Organismic perception does not shatter the box.

⟩   It stretches it.
⟩   It enlarges it.
⟩   It reorganizes it.

And it becomes more real.

What Active Awareness Is For

Allowing your system to register information more directly is not a party trick. It is not for prediction or spectacle.

It serves life. It allows you to:

⟩   navigate relationships with clarity rather than projection
⟩   sense misalignment before crisis
⟩   make decisions from coherence rather than fear
⟩   remain oriented in complexity
⟩   reduce distortion and overwhelm
⟩   live from a grounded center

This is perceptual maturity. When awareness matures in this way, life does not become abstract or detached.

Life Beyond the Box

To live beyond the box is not to abandon structure. It is to inhabit a larger structure, one capable of holding:

⟩   subtle information
⟩   symbolic meaning
⟩   emotional clarity
⟩   complexity without collapse

This was the aim of the perceptual system Ingo devoted his life to mapping: returning humans to their full perceptual bandwidth: grounded, coherent, ethical, and awake.

Not as a supernatural gift. As a natural birthright.

You began by noticing.

You end by living from what you notice.

AUTHOR'S ENDING NOTE

Note on Lineage

Before closing this series, it feels important to acknowledge the lineage of inquiry that helped shape its development.

The material presented throughout the *You Know More Than You Think* series is original and experiential in nature. It is not a restatement, continuation, or application of any single existing system or doctrine.

However, like all genuine inquiry, it did not arise in isolation.

This work emerged through sustained engagement with questions that have occupied scientists, philosophers, and observers of human experience for generations:

> How does perception organize reality?
> What determines what becomes knowable?
> How do structures of belief shape what can be seen?

Among the influences that sharpened these questions, my uncle Ingo's writings were particularly significant, not as a framework to adopt or a set of claims to accept, but as provocations that illuminated deeper lines of inquiry.

His work repeatedly returned to several themes that remain central to this series:

> how perception organizes experience
> how awareness conditions what becomes visible
> how limits to understanding arise from perceptual structure rather than from absence of information

The following works by Ingo were especially influential:

> **Everybody's Guide to Natural ESP**
> **Reality Boxes**
> **Secrets of Power, Volumes I & II**
> **Superpowers of the Human Biomind (essay series)**
> **The Wisdom Category**
> **Your Nostradamus Factor**

These writings are not prerequisites for engaging with this series. They are offered for readers who wish to explore one strand of the broader inquiry into perception and awareness that informed it.

Each book in this series also draws from a wide range of scientific and philosophical sources, acknowledged separately in its reference section.

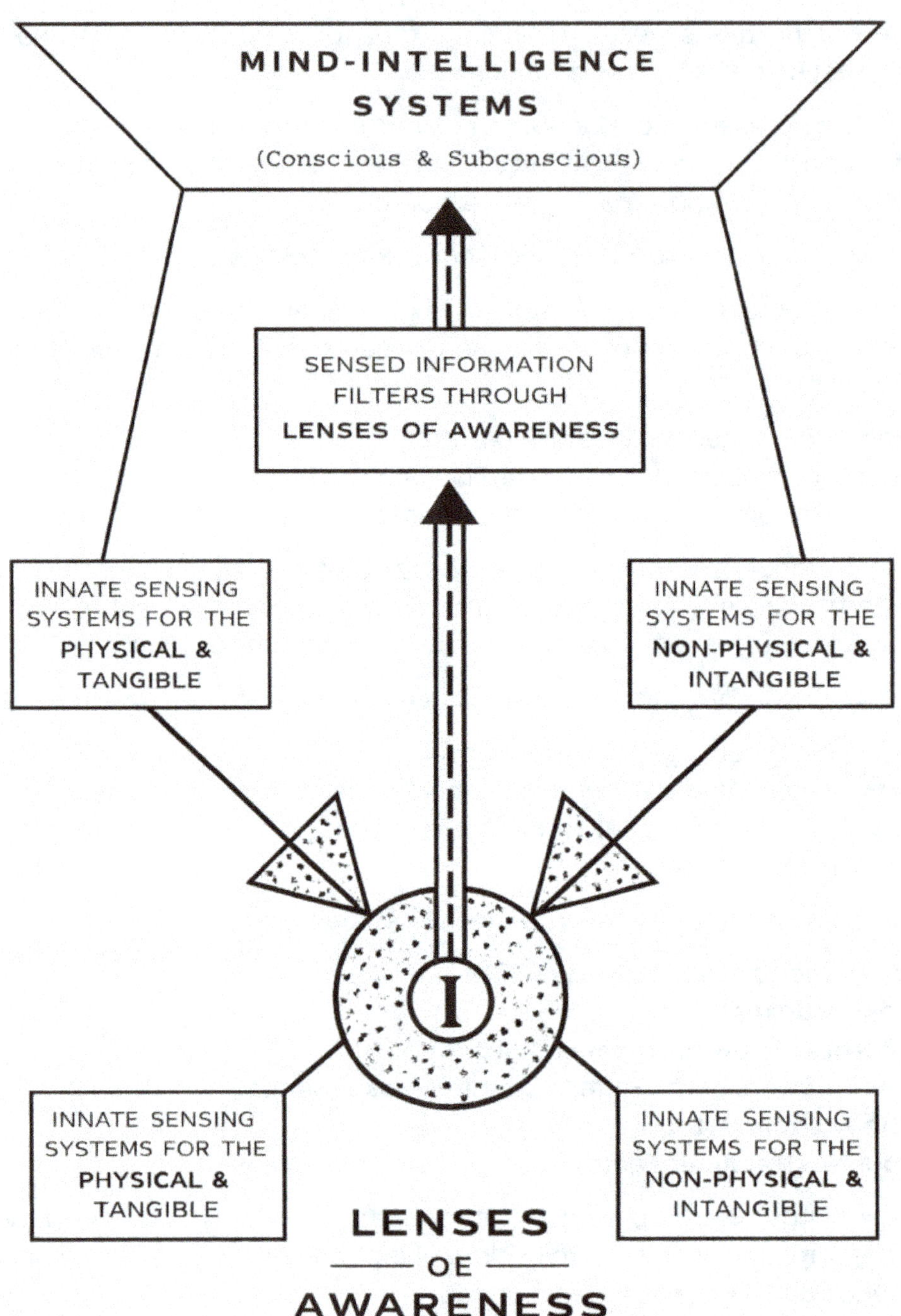

MIND-INTELLIGENCE SYSTEMS
(Conscious & Subconscious)
SENSED INFORMATION FILTERS THROUGH LENSES OF AWARENESS
INNATE SENSING SYSTEMS FOR THE PHYSICAL & TANGIBLE
INNATE SENSING SYSTEMS FOR THE NON-PHYSICAL & INTANGIBLE
I
INNATE SENSING SYSTEMS FOR THE PHYSICAL & TANGIBLE
INNATE SENSING SYSTEMS FOR THE NON-PHYSICAL & INTANGIBLE
LENSES OE AWARENESS

The Continuum of Knowledge: What Ingo Was Really Pointing Toward

In his later and more reflective writings (particularly in *The Wisdom Category*) Ingo pointed toward something larger than any single perceptual function or isolated human capacity.

He described what might be understood as a continuum of knowledge.

In this view, knowledge does not exist as a flat resource equally available to every state of mind. Instead, it unfolds across ranges of perception: from basic sensory information, to conceptual understanding, to symbolic recognition, and eventually to forms of wisdom that require correspondingly organized awareness to perceive.

One of his most consistent observations followed from this:

Knowledge associated with wider states of awareness cannot be understood from narrower ones.

Not because it is hidden.

But because one's organismic intelligence must develop the capacity to recognize it.

From this perspective, wisdom is not secreted away or deliberately withheld. It simply remains imperceptible until the internal conditions required to perceive it are present.

Symbolic Language and the Architecture of Knowing

Ingo often used metaphors that could sound unusual at first encounter: repositories of knowledge, guardians, shielding, access control, telepathy, luminous stores of understanding.

These images were not intended as literal descriptions of hidden vaults or supernatural archives. They were symbolic ways of describing how knowledge organizes itself.

Across cultures and eras, advanced knowledge is frequently represented as:

⟩ radiant
⟩ protected
⟩ vast
⟩ non-physical
⟩ accessible only through development

These archetypal images appear repeatedly because they mirror an internal truth:

Knowledge unfolds in layers, and one's system must mature in order to recognize deeper relationships.

Symbolic language often emerges where conceptual vocabulary reaches its limits.

A Continuing Inquiry

Awareness has always moved forward this way.

Not through institutions, declarations, or monuments, but through individuals who are willing (sometimes only briefly) to notice beyond the limits of what they have been told is *sensible*.

This series is not the conclusion of that inquiry.

It is an invitation to continue it.

Perception grows. And as perception grows, what can be known grows with it.

Because the structures that once shaped what you could see are no longer invisible.

What happens next does not belong to this book.

It belongs to what you notice.

Consciousness IS.

And it is bigger than you think.

—Ingo Swann, *Reality Boxes*

APPENDIX

Quick Reset Practices

The brief resets below are not techniques to master or practices to perform regularly. They are simple ways of returning your system to a workable state when it drifts, intensifies, or becomes unclear.

You may use them as needed, or not at all.

Body Reset
(returning to physical presence)

> Exhale longer than you inhale.
> Relax your shoulders.
> Feel a connection to the ground through your feet or seat.
> Drop into the present moment.

Boundary Reset
(restoring perceptual containment)

> Inhale → gently gather your attention to your perimeter.
> Exhale → allow your boundary to close.
> Focus on a soft containment around the body.

Coherence Reset
(stabilizing rhythm and tone)

> Inhale for 5 seconds.
> Exhale for 5 seconds.
> Bring to mind something you appreciate.
> Let your attention smooth and stabilize.

Emotional Check-In
(staying oriented with feeling)

> Where is the sensation located?
> What is its texture?
> What is its direction (up / down / inward / outward)?
> Can it soften with one breath?

Perceptual Reorientation
(returning to balanced attention)

> Turn your attention inward.
> Soften your visual focus.
> Allow your awareness to include the room around you.

SELECTED SCIENTIFIC & PHILOSOPHICAL FOUNDATIONS

The following works have informed the biological, cognitive, social, and phenomenological perspectives that shape this book.

They are not cited exhaustively, but represent foundational contributions in social cognition, motivated reasoning, predictive processing, collective perception, epistemology, cognitive bias, identity formation, and the neurobiology of awareness.

The explorations in this book draw upon established findings in attention, salience detection, identity-protective cognition, intergroup psychology, emotion regulation, group polarization, and perceptual filtering, alongside philosophical works that informed the conceptual development of these practices.

References

Aristotle. (1984). *On the soul* (J. A. Smith, Trans.). In J. Barnes (Ed.), *The complete works of Aristotle* (Vol. 1). Princeton University Press.

Barrett, L. F. (2017). *How emotions are made: The secret life of the brain.* Houghton Mifflin Harcourt.

Bikhchandani, S., Hirshleifer, D., & Welch, I. (1992). A theory of fads, fashion, custom, and cultural change as informational cascades. *Journal of Political Economy, 100*(5), 992–1026.

Blanke, O., & Metzinger, T. (2009). Full-body illusions and minimal phenomenal selfhood. *Trends in Cognitive Sciences, 13*(1), 7–13.

Bothmer, V., & Daglis, I. A. (2007). *Space weather: Physics and effects.* Springer.

Brehm, J. W. (1966). *A theory of psychological reactance.* Academic Press.

Carrington, R. C. (1860). Description of a singular appearance seen in the sun on September 1, 1859. *Monthly Notices of the Royal Astronomical Society, 20*, 13–15.

Central Intelligence Agency. (1976, January 14). Novel biophysical information transfer mechanisms (NBIT) (CIA-RDP79-00999A000300070001-4). Declassified intelligence report.

Chizhevsky, A. L. (1971). *Physical factors of the historical process* (Original work published 1924). Nauka.

Cicero. (1942). *De oratore* (E. W. Sutton & H. Rackham, Trans.). Harvard University Press. (Original work published 55 BCE).

Clark, A. (2016). *Surfing uncertainty: Prediction, action, and the embodied mind.* Oxford University Press.

Craig, A. D. (2002). Interoception and bodily awareness. *Nature Reviews Neuroscience, 3*(8), 655–666.

Critchley, H. D., & Garfinkel, S. N. (2017). Interoception and emotion. *Current Opinion in Psychology, 17*, 7–14.

Dane, E. (2010). Reconsidering the trade-off between expertise and flexibility: A cognitive entrenchment perspective. *Academy of Management Review, 35*(4), 579–603.

Defense Intelligence Agency. (1975, September). *Soviet and Czechoslovakian parapsychology research (U)* (CIA-RDP96-00792R000600350001-3). Declassified intelligence report.

Dubrov, A. P. (1978). *The geomagnetic field and life: Geomagnetobiology.* Plenum Press.

Dunlap, J. C., Loros, J. J., & DeCoursey, P. J. (2004). *Chronobiology: Biological timekeeping.* Sinauer Associates.

Festinger, L. (1957). *A theory of cognitive dissonance.* Stanford University Press.

Friston, K. (2010). The free-energy principle. *Nature Reviews Neuroscience, 11*(2), 127–138.

Gadamer, H.-G. (2004). *Truth and method* (2nd rev. ed., J. Weinsheimer & D. G. Marshall, Trans.). Continuum. (Original work published 1960).

Greenberg, J., Pyszczynski, T., & Solomon, S. (1986). The causes and consequences of a need for self-esteem: A terror management theory. In R. F. Baumeister (Ed.), *Public self and private self* (pp. 189–212). Springer.

Gross, J. J. (1998). The emerging field of emotion regulation. *Review of General Psychology, 2*(3), 271–299.

Haidt, J. (2012). *The righteous mind.* Pantheon.

Halliwell, S. (2002). *The aesthetics of mimesis: Ancient texts and modern problems.* Princeton University Press.

Hasher, L., Goldstein, D., & Toppino, T. (1977). Frequency and the conference of referential validity. *Journal of Verbal Learning and Verbal Behavior, 16*(1), 107–112.

Hohwy, J. (2013). *The predictive mind.* Oxford University Press.

Johnsen, S., & Lohmann, K. J. (2005). The physics and neurobiology of magnetoreception. *Nature Reviews Neuroscience, 6*(9), 703–712.

Jost, J. T., & Banaji, M. R. (1994). Stereotyping and system justification. *British Journal of Social Psychology, 33*(1), 1–27.

Kahan, D. M. (2013). Ideology and motivated reasoning. *Judgment and Decision Making, 8*(4), 407–424.

Kahan, D. M. (2017). Misconceptions, misinformation, and the logic of identity-protective cognition. *Yale Law School Public Law Research Paper No. 605.*

Kahneman, D. (2011). *Thinking, fast and slow.* Farrar, Straus and Giroux.

Kauffman, S. A. (1995). *At home in the universe: The search for laws of self-organization and complexity.* Oxford University Press.

Kirschvink, J. L., Shcherbakov, V. P., & Winklhofer, M. (2010). Magnetite-based magnetoreception. *Current Opinion in Neurobiology, 20*(3), 343–352.

Marvin, U. B. (2006). *The history of meteorites and the debate over their origin.* In D. S. Lauretta & H. Y. McSween Jr. (Eds.), Meteorites and the early solar system II (pp. 1–17). University of Arizona Press.

Mercier, H., & Sperber, D. (2017). *The enigma of reason.* Harvard University Press.

Metzinger, T. (2009). *The ego tunnel.* Basic Books.

Nickerson, R. S. (1998). Confirmation bias. *Review of General Psychology, 2*(2), 175–220.

Nguyen, C. T. (2020). Echo chambers and epistemic bubbles. *Episteme, 17*(2), 141–161.

Noelle-Neumann, E. (1993). *The spiral of silence: Public opinion—our social skin* (2nd ed.). University of Chicago Press.

Palumbo, R. V., et al. (2017). Interpersonal autonomic physiology. *Personality and Social Psychology Review, 21*(2), 99–141.

Persinger, M. A. (1987). *Neuropsychological bases of God beliefs.* Praeger.

Persinger, M. A. (1988). Geophysical variables and behavior: LXXXIII. Increased geomagnetic activity and the occurrence of exceptional experiences. *Perceptual and Motor Skills, 66*(2), 653–654.

Porges, S. W. (2011). *The polyvagal theory.* W. W. Norton.

Prentice, D. A., & Miller, D. T. (1993). Pluralistic ignorance and alcohol use on campus: Some consequences of misperceiving the social norm. *Journal of Personality and Social Psychology, 64*(2), 243–256.

Presman, A. S. (1970). *Electromagnetic fields and life.* Plenum Press.

Roenneberg, T., & Merrow, M. (2016). The circadian clock and human health. *Current Biology, 26*(10), R432–R443.

Schooler, J. W. (2002). Meta-consciousness and monitoring. *Trends in Cognitive Sciences, 6*(8), 339–344.

Schrijver, C. J., & Siscoe, G. L. (2010). *Heliophysics: Space storms and radiation.* Cambridge University Press.

Seeley, W. W., et al. (2007). Salience and executive control networks. *Journal of Neuroscience, 27*(9), 2349–2356.

Siegel, D. J. (2012). *The developing mind* (2nd ed.). Guilford Press.

Sunstein, C. R. (2009). *Going to extremes*. Oxford University Press.

Swann, I. (1977, August). *Psychic warfare* [Speech]. Harold Sherman's Mind–Body–Spirit Workshop, St. Louis, MO, United States.

Swann, I. (1996b). *Remote viewing — the real story: The discoveries, the political and technical history, the rise and fall, the saga, and the strange circumstances* [Autobiographical memoir]. Biomind Superpowers.

Swann, I. (1999, October 2). *Awareness and perception vs status of individual "realities".* Biomind Superpowers.

Swann, I. (2000). *Secrets of power, Volume I: Individual empowerment vs. the societal panorama of power and depowerment.* Ingo Swann Books.

Swann, I. (2002). *Secrets of power, Volume II: The vitalizing of individual powers.* Ingo Swann Books.

Swann, I. (2003a). *Reality boxes: And other black holes in human consciousness.* Ingo Swann Books.

Swann, I. (2003b). *The wisdom category: Shedding light on a lost light.* Ingo Swann Books.

Swann, I. (2018). *Psychic literacy: & the coming psychic renaissance.* Swann-Ryder Productions, LLC.

Tajfel, H., & Turner, J. C. (1979). Intergroup conflict theory. In W. G. Austin & S. Worchel (Eds.), *The social psychology of intergroup relations* (pp. 33–47). Brooks/Cole.

Thayer, J. F., & Lane, R. D. (2000). Neurovisceral integration. *Journal of Affective Disorders, 61*(3), 201–216.

Thompson, E. (2007). *Mind in life.* Harvard University Press.

Van Bavel, J. J., & Pereira, A. (2018). The partisan brain: An identity-based model of political belief. *Trends in Cognitive Sciences, 22*(3), 213–224.

www.ingramcontent.com/pod-product-compliance
Lightning Source LLC
Chambersburg PA
CBHW080447030726
47592CB00011B/3010

THE SERIES
You Are More Than You Think

Book One
What's Already There

Book Two
Where You Sit

Book Three
The Shape of Knowing

Book Four
Above the Noise

Book Five
The Gravity of Reality

Chapter numbers continue across volumes to reflect that the series unfolds as one integrated structure rather than as separate works. Each book stands on its own, but the numbering maintains the progression for readers who move across the entire sequence.

Elly Flippen is the niece of Ingo Swann and the editor of **Why Do We Feel There Is More to Us Than We, or Anyone, Knows About?**, as well as the author of **Conjunction.World.**

Her work is shaped by years of engagement with questions of perception, awareness, and the lived experience of human intelligence beyond habit and assumption.

She invites readers to rely on their own sensing and discernment, recognizing perception not as something to acquire, but as something already active and waiting to be understood.

To learn more about Ingo Swann and his work, visit **www.ingoswann.com.**